HAPPY
WOMEN
Live
Better

VALORIE
BURTON

HARVEST HOUSE PUBLISHERS
EUGENE, OREGON

Cover design by Harvest House Publishers Inc., Eugene, Oregon

Cover photo © Chris Garborg

Makeup by Kym Lee

Valorie Burton is represented by the literary agency of Alive Communications, Inc., 7680 Goddard Street, Ste #200, Colorado Springs, CO 80920. www.alivecommunications.com.

HAPPY WOMEN LIVE BETTER

Copyright © 2013 by Valorie Burton
Published by Harvest House Publishers
Eugene, Oregon 97402
www.harvesthousepublishers.com

Library of Congress Cataloging-in-Publication Data
Burton, Valorie, 1973-
Happy women live better / Valorie Burton.
    pages cm
ISBN 978-0-7369-5675-8 (pbk.)
ISBN 978-0-7369-5677-2 (eBook)
1. Women—Religious life. 2. Happiness—Religious aspects—Christianity. I. Title.
BV4527.B87 2013
248.8'43—dc23
                                        2013022684

Printed in the United States of America

13 14 15 16 17 18 19 20 21 / BP-CD / 10 9 8 7 6 5 4 3 2 1

*May the crossing of our paths lead you to
more smiles, more laughs, and more life!*

Contents

Happy Women
Read Introductions!

I know, I know. You like to go straight to the first chapter and skip the introduction. But this one time, don't. Before we dive in and discover how you can be happier starting today, I want to shed some light on why this subject matters at this point in history. And why your picking this book up is about more than just your happiness. It is about a movement.

We are in a crisis. But no one seems to have noticed. As women, we have more, but we enjoy less. We are more educated. We have more choices. We make more money. We raise fewer children. And thanks to technology, the chores are much easier. Women today have more opportunities than any women in the history of the world. And yet, research shows that collectively we are *less* happy than we were 40 years ago—while men are actually getting happier.[1] Why is that? And just as importantly, what can *you* do about it so you don't fall into these alarming statistics? Here are just a few of them:

- While we were told we could "have it all," and it is assumed we all want to climb the highest heights of professional success, three quarters of working women today say they aspire to a financial lifestyle that would allow them to stop working and stay home.[2]

- Women today are twice as likely to be depressed as men.[3]

- Today, the average age of the first onset of depression is ten years younger than it was just a generation ago.[4]

- Women who pursue "it all" (education, career, marriage, children) have increasingly discovered that the more they achieve in the first half of that equation (education, career), the smaller their chances of success in the second half (marriage, children). Statistics are clear that the more educated you are and the more money you make, the less likely you are to ever get married and have children. The opposite is true for men.[5]

I have written this book with a dual mission in mind: to get women talking about their happiness and to give you the tools to be happier.

My conversations with women from all walks of life echo the same refrain, whether they have a stellar career and no kids or are married, stay-at-home moms of five: "I should be doing more." "This isn't what I thought life would be." "I feel like I'm missing out on something." In this book you'll hear from women like you, talking about the angst they feel in life. The pressure they feel to catch up. The disappointment they feel at having done the right things and checked the right boxes, and somehow still not getting the life they'd expected. And you'll hear from some who somehow seem to "have it all." What's their secret? I think you'll be surprised by the answers.

Mission #1: What's Going On?

First, I want to spark conversation between you and your girlfriends, daughters, aunties, cousins, coworkers, and any woman in your circle. As women, we need to raise our consciousness about the impact of cultural shifts on our collective happiness. Why does high income decrease a woman's prospects for marriage and family? Why do men get happier as they get older while many women tend to get sadder—and how can you keep that from being your story? And can you really "have it all"—and how do you define "having it all"?

Through multiple conversations and taking a look at the growing research, it has become obvious to me that the threat to women's happiness has been gradual. Because of that, most of us have not noticed the changes in expectations and dynamics over the last 40 years or so that have dramatically increased our stress levels and made it harder to achieve happiness. Women who were young adults in the late 1960s and early 1970s point out the differences in cultural expectations easily. Having lived it and watched the changes over time, the contrast is stark.

"In 1972, there were fewer expectations on anybody about anything!" pointed out Christine Duvivier, positive psychologist and parenting expert. "I don't think there were as many expectations on anybody about what you were supposed to achieve or supposed to have."

Whatever the reasons for the shifts in our culture—changes that are likely impacting you in ways you may not have previously considered—you can be a part of the solution. You can raise awareness merely by bringing up the subject. I promise. *Every woman has an opinion about it.*

As I stumbled across this topic, I simply brought it up casually to every woman I came in contact with. "Did you know research shows that since the early 1970s women have become less happy while men are getting happier? Especially by their early 40s, many women are feeling like life just hasn't turned out to be all they'd hoped. They've tried to have it all, but too many come up short. Why do you think that is?" Not one woman responded, "I don't know." Instead, they launched into long diatribes about their own lives, their daughters, their mothers, their friends. The comments were wide-ranging, but shared a similar theme:

I'm exhausted trying to do it all.

I feel like I've never done enough.

I feel guilty that I don't do more.

One spring morning while sitting at Starbucks in Rockefeller Center after appearing as a guest on the *Today Show*, I met with producers from the *Dr. Oz* show. I'd previously appeared on their show and one of the producers asked what I was working on now. I started talking about this book and began to share the themes women were sharing with me. The two producers chimed in, sharing opinions from their own lives and families. Out of the blue, a perfect stranger approached our table. She looked a little scattered and quite interested in telling us something. In her British accent she said, "Excuse me. I don't normally eavesdrop on conversations, but what you're talking about is so fascinating and so true." Then for the next ten minutes she eagerly explained the stress of working, commuting, and being a wife and a mom. "I think it's just a myth that you can have it all," she said, sounding frustrated and like she just needed someone to hear that. "I don't even want it all. I wish I could just stay home, but I can't. We need the money."

She isn't alone in her angst. Consider some of these comments from women I interviewed:

- A 43-year-old mom of six, married 18 years and now embarking on a career in ministry, said, "I just feel so behind. I feel like I should have gotten started ten years ago."

- A 26-year-old newlywed shared, "I feel so much pressure to get it right—at work, at home. Everyone is asking when we will have kids. I don't know! Right now, I'm just trying to figure out how to be married and have a career at the same time."

- A 38-year-old single professional shared, "I feel judged so often, like people think I exchanged having a family for having a great career. Truth is, I want it all. I thought I'd be married by now. It hasn't happened. I'm starting to wonder if it ever will. I am usually strong in my faith so I feel guilty about my doubts."

- A 60-year-old mom of two chimed in: "I think young women are stressed today because they have so many expectations on them. When I finished high school, the expectation was that I'd get married and have a family, maybe become a secretary. I felt no pressure whatsoever to conquer the world."

The last comment by the Baby Boomer mom may just have hit the nail on the head. With more choices than ever before comes more opportunity for second-guessing and regret. With higher expectations come more opportunities to disappoint and fail. With more women than ever climbing the ladder of professional and financial success comes more opportunities for comparison—and the chance to feel guilty that somehow you are not doing enough. Multiple challenges can contribute to feelings that deplete happiness and contentment. And through these pages, I want us to start a much-needed conversation about it.

Start the Conversation

If you were drawn to something about this book, I believe you are one of the women with the ability to spark the conversation across this nation. Women want to be happy, but more and more women are finding authentic happiness to be elusive—all the while putting on a smile to mask the disappointment, discouragement, and frustration of doing things they thought would bring happiness only to discover they don't. We'll dive into some important questions—questions that have an impact on just how happy of a life you live.

- Why is it more difficult to be content today than just a few decades ago—and getting even harder with time?
- When have you done enough?
- Didn't our moms tell us we could have it all? Were they making that up or were we just the first generation to embark on the great experiment to find out?

The first step to conquering a challenge is recognizing it exists. So we'll peel back the layers of the many changes in society that have created unexpected dynamics in the lives of women. Most importantly, we'll talk about what those changes mean to *you* and what you can do to ensure your own happiness.

Mission #2: What's Your Happiness Trigger?

The other mission of this book is helping you get happier. Using pioneering research from the field of positive psychology—the study of what makes us happier, healthier, and more resilient—I've identified 13 happiness triggers. Every happiness trigger can boost your happiness, but you have "signature triggers," happiness instigators that are more likely than others to produce positive emotion for you. We will explore each of the 13 happiness triggers and how you can activate them in your everyday life to live more joyfully and authentically, less stressed, and more satisfied. I've designed an assessment that will tell you what your strongest happiness triggers are. You can take it for free online at www.happywomantest.com.

Not only will you learn what your strongest happiness triggers are, but throughout these pages, I will share specific activities that will help you put your triggers to work. While many books exist on happiness, to my knowledge, none has ever discussed the concept of happiness triggers and the fact that what makes you happiest may be entirely different from what makes another happiest. The key to unlocking your authentic happiness may indeed lie in getting clarity about what innately energizes you and brings you the deepest level of meaning and satisfaction. Learning this now can create revolutionary change in your life—and it can help your friends, mate, and loved ones better understand what makes you unique. Likewise, I encourage you to have those closest to you take the assessment. Imagine what it can do for your relationships to better understand the happiness triggers of your children, spouse, friends, coworkers, and family members. Having this deeper understanding of what triggers happiness in yourself and others is bound to produce exciting results in your relationships.

How the Book Is Laid Out

Happiness Triggers

There are 13 happiness triggers you will learn in this book. They are skills, really. Happiness is a skill. If you practice the habits of happiness and make more choices that lead to happiness and fewer that don't, you'll see the amount of joy and contentment in your life measurably increase. In fact, studies show that while half of your happiness is genetic, only ten percent is based on your circumstances.[6] The apostle Paul was right when he declared, "I have learned the secret of being content in any and every situation…whether living in plenty or in want" (Philippians 4:12). About 40 percent of happiness is what you do intentionally.[7] It is about your everyday habits, your relationships, and how you spend your time. Happiness triggers serve as a guide for how to influence that 40 percent. I'll share these skills with you, give you a road map to use them, and vivid examples of how other women have used them to create more happiness and joy in their lives.

Conversation Starters

Between each happiness trigger, you'll find a conversation starter. These chapters are meant to point out the cultural shifts and dynamics that really impact you and your ability to be happy—even if you haven't noticed. You'll be challenged to talk about these conversation starters with others and develop your own plan of action for how to keep these dynamics from draining your joy.

You'll see questions at the start of each conversation starter that you can use for discussion with friends and getting clearer about your own growth and fulfillment. They are meant to facilitate chats and banter with the women in your life to get you all talking about that particular happiness trigger and how you can activate it—and what could hinder it from taking shape in your life. And even when you don't discuss the questions with others, I encourage you to explore your answers to the questions. In doing so, you will begin to intentionally shape your thoughts and opinions in a way that empowers you to own your happiness.

My goal is that you finish this book equipped with the tools to be happier and that you will gain an increased awareness of the cultural factors that you must encounter along your journey. The cultural factors are sometimes going to seem a bit negative. I wish that weren't so, but it is the reality we face. The good news is that there is plenty you can do about it.

12 Happiness Myths Every Woman Should Know

Just one more thing before we dive in. There are a few assumptions—let's call them myths—that many of us buy into when it comes to happiness. Let's just go ahead and debunk them now. Some are surprising. Some you may resist. Raising your awareness about them expands your toolbox of happiness knowledge so that you can make decisions and set expectations that serve you and help you to be happy on your way to your life's vision rather than simply holding your breath until you arrive.

1. You know what will make you happy.

"If only" is a phrase that causes many women to stumble on the road to happiness. But research actually confirms that we are pretty poor predictors of what will make us happy. It's the sad truth. We think the relationship will make us happy. The new job will make us happy. Being in charge will make us happy. But the truth is, happiness is a state of mind. What makes you happy is your attitude toward your life. In fact, happiness has been defined as "how you *feel* about the life you are living." It is subjective. And if you can't be happy while you don't have everything you want, you likely won't be happy when you get everything you want. Because if happiness is about checking off your list of things and people you need to arrive at happiness, the list will magically keep growing.

2. Success produces happiness.

Pretty much everything we pursue in life we pursue because we believe it will make us happier—whether it's love or a career or weight loss or money. Success is no different. But the myth that success produces happiness is simply untrue. It is actually the other way around. The attitude, positive emotion, and optimism that accompany happiness create success. Studies show that happier people are more likely to get promoted, make more money, and persevere in the face of challenges.

3. Happiness is about what happens.

It's a catchy phrase and it seems to make sense: "Happiness is about what happens to you." But it isn't true. Circumstances actually account for just ten percent of your happiness. Study after study shows that after difficult or even tragic circumstances, people bounce back to levels of happiness close to where they were prior to the change in circumstances. So a miserable person remains miserable and a fairly happy person adjusts to the new circumstances and regains happiness.

4. *Focusing on happiness is selfish.*

"There is nothing better for people than to be happy and do good while they live…this is the gift of God," King Solomon proclaims in the Old Testament book of Ecclesiastes. So why do so many people of faith think that focusing on happiness is "selfish"? Truth is, happiness is good for your health and it's contagious. What better way to live your life than to journey through it with a positive attitude and level of happiness that lifts others?

5. *With so many more opportunities and advances in the workplace and society, women are happier today than they were 40 years ago.*

I'd love to be able to tell you this is true, but it isn't. Women today report lower levels of happiness than women in 1972, and men actually report higher levels of happiness. Worse yet, on average, women get sadder and less fulfilled as they get older while men report feeling more fulfilled.

6. *Women who work are happier and more fulfilled.*

I almost hate to say it, but this also is not true. Women who stay at home report greater happiness than those who work. I don't find this particularly shocking. As much as I love what I do and know I'm living in my purpose, there are days I daydream about not working at all. Can you relate? Fulfillment can be found in many ways, and millions of women have found it without 9 to 5.

7. *Having children will make you happier.*

This is by no means to suggest you shouldn't have children, but multiple studies over multiple decades show that married women with children are less happy than married women without children. For that matter, you can imagine that single moms report higher stress levels and less happiness than single women without children. Children are a gift from God, but in today's world, they also bring a level of stress and anxiety that impacts happiness.

8. If I could just make more money, I'd be happier.

There are actually only a few ways money will make you happier. And beyond a household income of $75,000 annually in the United States, increases in happiness are very small.[8] If you are living in poverty—let's say $15,000 per year—and get a boost to $45,000 per year, your happiness will skyrocket. That's because getting your needs met is essential for happiness. But once needs are met, money is not the biggest determinant of happiness. Giving some away will make you happier. So will living below your means.

9. If I live in the best neighborhood, I'll be happier.

Actually, you'll be happier in a neighborhood that is a bit less than you can afford. It turns out we are happier when living in an environment where we are doing at least slightly better than those around us. It decreases the pressure of "keeping up with the Jones." As a result, you are less likely to feel like you are missing out, underachieving, or falling behind, all of which are good for your happiness.

10. Marriage makes women happier and men feel confined.

You've seen the stereotype on every sitcom. The married man complains about how he has to get his wife's permission to go out with the fellas or is frustrated by his wife's nagging or incessant honey-do list. You kinda get the idea that men are dragged into marriage kicking and screaming. And the women, of course, are all just dying to get married. It is an intriguing cultural stereotype because study after study shows that men are actually happier in marriage than women. And when men divorce, they are more likely than women to remarry—and they remarry faster than women.

11. Happiness is easy.

Uhh…not in the world we live in today. We are constantly bombarded with messages that tell us we can't be happy until we get the promotion, the relationship, the house, the perfect body. And we have fewer of the support systems in place that facilitate happiness—family nearby, neighbors we know, low expenses—and expectations to match.

12. *"Having it all" will make you happy.*

This is up for debate. By the looks of things, more and more women are opting out of trying—or have tried and just can't seem to "have it all" even if they want to. Forty-three percent of Generation X women who are college graduates don't have children. Of the ones who do, record numbers are opting to leave the workforce and stay home with their kids. And the ones who are working and raising children face stressors and challenges that erode happiness. This is not to say there are no women who "have it all," but achieving "it all"—the husband, kids, stellar career, knockout body, and happiness—requires an alignment of circumstances few women have.

So how about you? Which of these myths have you bought into? And how does it impact your feelings about where you are in your life? In this book, I invite you to drop the myths and start over with a new concept of what it takes to be happy. It is about renewing your mind and washing away all the beliefs that actually sabotage your happiness and learning the skills of happiness that actually work. Using a combination of powerful research, biblical wisdom, stories from real women, and conversation starters for you and your friends, we are about to begin a journey that can transform your life.

You ready? Let's get started.

Anticipation

How to use the power of positive
expectation to boost your mood

Decision

"Every day, I make sure I have something to look forward to."

S ingle and down in the dumps over the seeming lack of eligible, desirable potential mates in her city, Shawn complained about her eventless weekends and lonely weeknights.

"I just want someone to do things with," she said during a coaching session. "Is that too much to ask?"

Well, maybe not. She's attractive and smart, and one would assume she doesn't have trouble getting a date. Her question is one most women in her position might ask. But I had a more important question for Shawn. "Rather than waiting for someone to show up and give you a 'reason' to do interesting and fun things," I said, "why not do interesting and fun things regardless of whether you have someone to do them with?"

"Well, I don't feel comfortable going places alone," she explained.

"Okay, so don't go alone. Ask a friend to go with you," I said.

Shawn paused. As simple a request as I was making, somehow it fell on Shawn like new information. She normally waited for friends to invite her to do things, but never made plans and invited others along. No wonder she was bored! Her life experience was not her own—it was by happenstance. Whatever experiences others created and invited her to be a part of, she did—from her work projects to one-year-old birthday parties. But whatever she attended, it was never her idea.

I challenged Shawn to proactively plan something interesting to do the following week. She accepted the challenge with enthusiasm, and noted that her attitude was indeed a little rigid when it came to planning something to look forward to. That week, a group she'd been meaning to get involved with had a gathering at a local restaurant and Shawn invited a colleague along. In a quick turn of events, Shawn met a gentleman that evening. Within a few weeks, a relationship began.

Now, I'm not suggesting that if you take one step, you'll find the love of your life. But I will say this: Once you take control of your life by creating anticipation—something to look forward to—you'll be surprised how many other welcome shifts can occur.

Shawn soon began putting the power of anticipation in her everyday life. She asked friends to dinner. She planned long bubble baths. She savored book night, when she curled up in bed early with a good book. She took a winetasting class and invited her sister to come along and joined a Saturday morning bike riding club she'd heard about through a colleague at work. Nearly every day, there was something to look forward to on her calendar.

If I took a look at the next seven days on your schedule, how much of it would you say is stuff you can't wait to do? Happiness, to a great extent, is having something to look forward to. It is savoring what's coming up. Be willing to get excited—even about that piece of cake you've held off all week to eat or that friend you finally carved out time to see tomorrow. The happiness trigger of anticipation is easy to pull off, but you must be intentional about it. In other words, you must do one of two things:

- Notice what's already in front of you to look forward to.
- Create something to look forward to.

When I was growing up, my parents always told me if I was bored, it was my fault. It meant I was waiting on someone else to entertain me rather than using my own creativity to find something constructive and interesting to do with my time. As adults, we often aren't bored (there's too much to do to be bored!), but we can fall into the rut of routine, feeling that every day is nothing but a series of to-do's to be checked off. How often do you wake up genuinely excited about the day ahead? What would it take to make that your reality?

Notice What's in Front of You

Maybe you can relate to this. Sometimes, when my calendar gets really full, I can get into a rut of dreading what's coming up. Mind you, I have spent years building a life that I actually love, so it is rare that I have something on the calendar that I didn't at some point actually *want* to do. But when there is too much of it, I forget about the fact that it's exciting stuff and begin to focus simply on the fact that there is so much of it. So I've learned to pause when I look at my calendar and then breathe, mindfully soaking in the upcoming events of the day. It's not just "stuff to do." It's my life. And I'm grateful for it. And most of it is something to look forward to.

When life becomes a crowded routine of work, obligations, and whatever else is on your overloaded plate, it dampens your joy. What are you looking forward to today? How about next week? Or three months from now? Research shows that anticipation—enthusiasm for a future event—increases positive emotion and boosts your happiness. But when your schedule is full and life has become a monotony of daily tasks and expectations, anticipation and enthusiasm are likely not the emotions you feel. The good news is this: You can intentionally create something to look forward to every single day. In fact, if you are going to be a happy woman, you must. Most happy women do this naturally. They may not even recognize it on a conscious level, but if you ask them about their schedule, you'll notice joy-inducing events sprinkled throughout their days and weeks.

So that meeting you have at 11 a.m.? Rather than another meeting, look at it as an opportunity to move forward and be productive. That lunch date you scheduled that you feel like you don't have time for today? Savor the time to slow down for a meal and connect with that person one-on-one in the midst of a full day. The gymnastics practice you must rush your daughter to later this afternoon? Remember the day when you dreamed of having a child of your own and savor the fact that you have a healthy, energetic little girl who is blossoming right before your eyes. Oh, and the finale of your favorite show you're going to curl up on the sofa and watch at 9 o'clock tonight? Express to somebody how much you're looking forward to it. Expression is a key to anticipation.

Multiply the Positive Emotions

Anticipation is about stirring up positive emotions about the future. In fact, when anticipation is done right, you can get as much positive emotion out of your anticipation of an event as you do from the event itself. It fits the old adage, "It's about the journey, not the destination." Planning your vacation is a perfect example of this, from perusing travel websites with vivid pictures of paradise destinations and imagining yourself there to booking your flight and talking through what you are looking forward to once you arrive. If it's a family or group vacation, plan a get-together weeks before the vacation to talk through plans and start your countdown. Every opportunity to generate excitement and joy in anticipation of an event multiplies your positive emotion.

If There's Nothing to Look Forward to, Create Something!

You might be like Shawn. If you look at your schedule, and don't see much to look forward to, it's time to be intentional and get creative. What have you been talking about doing for the longest? Maybe it's time to make it happen. Is there a milestone you've recently reached or one that's coming up? Come up with a way to celebrate it. Whether it's a small acknowledgment (you'll treat yourself to that new pair of shoes you've been eyeing!) or big bash (so what if you've never thrown a bash—this'll be your first!), celebration fosters anticipation.

The Power of Novelty: Try Something New

One exciting way to have something to look forward to is to try something new. Novelty boosts happiness by keeping your life from becoming dull. Always fresh with some new activity or learning, you look forward to the next adventure. Recently, I decided I want to try growing some food. This has always intrigued me. Although I spent my summers with my grandparents and my grandmother had a half-acre garden with corn, cabbage, beets, green beans, potatoes, tomatoes, and squash and a large backyard with an apple tree, plum trees, peach trees, blackberry bushes, and more, I never had a clue how all that stuff managed to sprout from the ground. As an adult, and especially now that "organic" is so popular, I've wondered just how Grandmama did it. So I started very simply—with patio tomatoes.

Just today, I picked my first ripe husky red cherry tomato. I know I sound like a commercial saying this, but it was fresh and bursting with flavor! Every morning, I look forward to going out to water my tomatoes. I wonder how many more are beginning to turn from green to orange and from orange to red. I get excited to see new baby tomatoes sprouting from the vine. And there is a sense of gratification I feel from knowing that I helped nurture them into existence. I thought growing food was more complicated than this! I learned something new. It makes me happy.

Everyday Anticipation: Thank God It's Monday!

Another powerful way to boost your happiness through the power of anticipation is to choose a career and workplace environment you absolutely love. With work taking up such a large percentage of most women's time today, having something to look forward to when you head to work is powerful. Consider this scenario from my own life:

I spent last New Year's Day on the beach in Miami. I got every ounce of joy out of my 12-day sabbatical—Christmastime with family, rest, play, and napping to the sound of the Atlantic's waves crashing on the South Florida shore. In fact, I didn't get back until New Year's night. I fussed at myself (well, in my head, I fussed) as the wheels touched down at Atlanta's Hartsfield-Jackson Airport. "Why didn't I close the office on January 2 too?" I thought.

While a buffer day to get back into the rhythm of things would have been nice, my spirit felt rejuvenated and excited about the New Year. I was ready to get back to work. So on January 2, I headed to the office. Just as I pulled up, I received this text from my assistant: *Soooo...* *per the calendar you are supposed to be off today. Just letting you know.*

Had I known, I'd still have been in bed. But I was dressed (in an outfit I'd thoughtfully picked out, no less!) and ready to rock. So I got out of the car and headed into the office. When my dad called mid-day, puttering around the house because he was off all week, I told him the story.

"I was supposed to be off today too, but I didn't realize it until I was already here!"

His response was echoed by several others as I jokingly recounted my dilemma that day: "Wow, now that's passion. It's obvious you really love what you do when you go to work even though you scheduled one more day off!"

Funny, I hadn't thought of it that way, but it's true. *I love what I do*. And I'm grateful. That wasn't always the case. At one point, I felt miserable in my previous career. I was good at it, but not at all passionate about it. I made a deliberate decision in 1999 to find my purpose and pursue it. Despite my worst fears that I somehow might not make a living at it (getting paid to "inspire" people isn't exactly on *Forbes'* "Top 10 Jobs" list), I went for it. My worst fears did not come true. But my dreams did. By 2001, I was doing it full-time.

Are you doing what you love for a living? If not, will you make a plan to start? Making a dream come true begins with this simple thought: *It's possible.*

In the beginning, you don't have to know exactly how to make it happen. You just need to believe it's possible and start moving in the right direction, asking the sort of questions that will lead you onto a new path. Make a decision to do what you love. Start small. Start now. I started part-time while I was running my own public relations agency. The road hasn't always been smooth, but it has been absolutely worth it. There's nothing like getting up in the morning excited about the day ahead, knowing you are going to make a positive impact on somebody. It's fun to be able to say, "Thank God it's Monday!"

Savor the Moment When It Arrives

Anticipation is savoring the future, but there are two other ways to savor that will make creating something to look forward to all the more worthwhile: savoring the moment and then reminiscing about it. Once you've spent time anticipating the experience, make sure you actually *enjoy* the experience. In our text-happy, social-media saturated culture, there is a temptation that didn't used to exist—the temptation to tell everybody what you're up to while you're up to it! Resist the urge. Fully engage in your moment once it arrives. Cherish it. Feel it. Taste it. Savor it. This moment will never come again.

Savor the Past Once the Moment Is Gone

When I was a little girl in Panama City, Florida, I looked forward with great anticipation to getting to play in the backyard. It wasn't just any backyard. Somehow, we lucked out. We lived on an Air Force base and our house just happened to be on the side of the street that backed up to the Gulf of Mexico. The view was spectacular. So at five or six years old, one of my favorite pastimes was sitting on my swing set in the middle of the backyard and watching the dolphins jump and play around three large poles about 100 yards from the water's edge. I'd count the number of dolphins and number of jumps. I'd get excited when they jumped completely over a pole rather than just bobbing out of the water. It was a real treat for me when the dolphins decided to play.

Just a few months before I turned seven years old, my parents brought me into the kitchen to explain that we were moving. I didn't really comprehend the concept at first—it had never occurred to me that we'd live anywhere other than where we were. And we weren't just moving down the street or even to another city. We were moving to another country: West Germany. As the time neared for us to move, my six-year-old mind decidedly wanted to forever remember what it felt like to sit in the blissfulness of that backyard ritual. Somehow, even at that young age, I knew how special it was. I recall sitting on my swing, telling myself the year and the place and taking a mental snapshot of the beautiful view in front of me. Even now, decades later, I can close my eyes and feel transported to that joyful moment in time.

Think back to a vivid, specific moment in your life when you were filled with joy. What happened? How did you feel? Who were you with? Savoring is a powerful way to induce positive emotion. There are three ways we savor: the past, present, and future. Although anticipation is about savoring the future, it is worthy to note that you can also generate positive emotion by savoring the moments you once anticipated. Whether it is a mental snapshot, a photographic snapshot, or a conversation spent reminiscing about a special moment, savoring the past is one way to extend the joy beyond the moment.

Positive Anticipation Versus Negative Anticipation

In the context of happiness, anticipation is positive. However, let's acknowledge that sometimes anticipation can be absolutely a negative. It can produce anxiety (negative). These days, I rarely get nervous before I speak. But when I do, I can always trace it to one thing: the thought that somehow the speaking engagement will go terribly, I won't connect with the audience, and the people who brought me in will be sorely disappointed. This has never actually happened, but somehow the thought would creep in and suddenly, I became anxious. One of my favorite pieces of advice comes from the apostle Paul, who said, "Do not worry about anything, but in everything by prayer and supplication with thanksgiving let your requests be made known to God" (Philippians 4:6). Coach yourself with this question: What outcome do I *want* to happen?

Five Simple Ways to Build Anticipation

1. Set a goal.

It is impossible to be happy without goals. Now, your goal doesn't have to be to conquer the world. But your life needs an aim. "This week, I'm going to jog a total of 10 miles." "Next year, we are going to take our dream vacation to Paris." "In five years, I'm going to be completely out of debt." Set meaningful goals with a reasonable timeline. Close your eyes and imagine yourself achieving the goal.

2. Make a list of simple pleasures.

It's easiest to activate the happiness trigger of anticipation if you don't have to always come up with ideas on the spot. Instead, set aside a few minutes to make a list of simple pleasures. You might even write them on individual small pieces of paper and put them in an anticipation jar. Then pull one out whenever it's time to add something new to your calendar.

3. Talk about it.

Don't keep your excitement to yourself. What are you most looking forward to? Share with a friend. Talk about why it's meaningful to you. Verbalize what it's going to feel like when the moment comes.

4. Add to the joy.

When you're intentional and you begin talking about something you're looking forward to, something fun happens. You start to think of ways you can make the moment even more meaningful. Maybe you invite someone to join you. Perhaps you incorporate other happiness triggers to multiply the effect. For example, you create something to look forward to that you've never done before (happiness trigger: novelty) or you surprise someone in need with something that will really bless them and savor their reaction (service). Get creative. Add to the joy.

5. Count down.

Remember when you were a kid and you knew exactly how many days were left until school was out for the summer? Much of the fun was in the countdown. The same is true with intentionally creating anticipation. Be a kid about it. Count down. Write it on the whiteboard in your office or change out a sticky note on the refrigerator or bathroom mirror every day. The moment is getting closer every day.

Who pushes your anticipation trigger?

As long as we're talking about having something to look forward to, why not apply it to your relationships? Ideally, you should surround yourself with people you look forward to spending time with—that should be a no-brainer! For those relationships you choose—friends or a mate, for example—a good measure of whether that relationship gives you energy or drains it is whether you actually look forward to being in the presence of that person. If you want to be happier, make it your goal to be around people who push your "anticipation" trigger. If they don't, ask yourself, "How could we enhance this relationship so that we look forward to seeing each other?" As you probably know, some people in your life are simply not going to change. And that may mean you need to set some boundaries. There are few things more powerful to effect our happiness than our relationships.

Lower the Expectation, Lower Your Anxiety

This is a little counterintuitive, but I have to touch on it. It is possible to go overboard with a happiness trigger. Any strength, when overused, can become a weakness. If you have a tendency toward overachievement, it can be easy to set expectations for yourself that create more stress than good. In fact, anticipation can also be about giving yourself permission to lower the bar a little. I'm going to let that soak in for a second. Think for a moment about the thing that you pressure yourself most about right now. There's so much expectation in it that it's like a balloon that's been filled to capacity with the air of expectation. Put any more air in there and it'll pop! Everything would have to come together absolutely perfectly in order for the expectation to be met. Oh, and you have a deadline on it too—and it's not a leisurely deadline, either. You got that thing in mind?

Now, close your eyes. Take a deep breath. And imagine that you gave yourself a little more breathing room with that goal. You'd still love for it to all come together the way you want, but loosen your grip on how it has to look. You reflect on the words of Jesus: "For my yoke is easy and my burden is light" (Matthew 11:30).

When our expectations of what must happen begin to line up in the perfect will of God for our lives, it isn't a burden. The yoke is easy.

High expectations create pressure and increase the likelihood of disappointment. Now, this is not to say you shouldn't have high expectations. However, be intentional about what you choose to have high expectations about. If your expectations are high about everything, the likelihood of disappointment and stress is much higher. If some of those expectations are about things that are not really all that meaningful, then you've unnecessarily caused yourself stress and disappointment. The goal is to activate happiness, not stress.

Activate This Happiness Trigger!

- Take a look at your calendar for the next week. What do you have to look forward to? How could you further enhance your enjoyment of those activities? If there's nothing to look forward to, what can you create and add to your schedule?

- Pause. Close your eyes. Breathe deeply. Now imagine your enjoyment of the activity you are most looking forward to. This is called anticipatory savoring.

- Talk about what you're looking forward to. Anticipation is not to be kept to yourself. Expressing your excitement for what you're anticipating—no matter how small or large—is a key activating this happiness trigger.

- Savor the moment. When the activity arrives, be fully present. Don't let distractions muffle your enjoyment.

- Remember it with fondness. Reminiscing about past pleasures is savoring the past. What did you enjoy most? How did it feel? What did it mean to you? Talk about it. And keep a journal. Writing in a journal is a great way to reflect on meaningful pleasures. And whenever you want a boost of positive emotion, you can always go back to your journal and savor a bit more! Or make a scrapbook or photo album (online works too!) to remember your experience by.

- Set a new, meaningful goal and describe what it will feel like to reach that goal.

- Make a list of simple pleasures. Then choose one to put on your calendar today.

CONVERSATION STARTER:

You Should Have It All, Right?

The high expectations and stress of being
a woman in the 21st century

- How do you define "having it all"?
- Do you ever feel like you are behind in life, as though you some-how missed the boat and are trying to catch up? In what way?
- What would it take for you to choose happiness right now, even if you can't currently check off all of the expectations on your "having it all" list?

At some point, the message of the women's movement seems to have shifted from "You can have it all" to "You *should* have it all." It became an expectation. And it's a lot of pressure. So you could be doing just great—perhaps you're raising your kids and doing a good job, but you left the workplace to focus on your family. "I feel like I'm behind," one mother of six told me. "I mean, I wanted to write a book by now. I just don't have much by way of career accomplishments," she explained. I sat across the table, baffled. She had a successful marriage of twenty years and six respectful, healthy, happy children. What an accomplishment! And yet even she felt the weight of the expectation to have it all—and all at the same time. Here's the "all" most women today have been taught and believe they are supposed to achieve:

- Successful career
- Adoring, handsome, successful husband
- Cute, admirable children
- Flawless looks

- Financial abundance
- Domestic perfection
- Happiness

With all the advances that have occurred in the last half century—from career options to birth control and fertility treatments to technology that puts the world at your fingertips—the choices are abundant. An abundance of choice can create a kind of stress women of previous generations didn't have.

Presumably "having it all" refers to having everything most women had a few decades ago (marriage, family) *and* the things men had that women didn't (equal opportunities in education, income, and career choices). In the meantime, men were not fighting to "have it all" (meaning everything they already had *plus the responsibilities of children and home*). So as the doors of opportunity opened for women outside the home, we took some of the load off of men. However, the expectation that women would be the primary caretakers of children and run the household remained. Meanwhile, the expectation of men as the sole provider all but disappeared—today, the dual income household is the norm. And some would say that while most women still aspire to marry and have a family, the pressure on men to do so early in life has declined.

Perhaps it is time to quit asking, "Can women have it all?" We know the answer to that question. *Yes, we can.* A handful even seem to make it look easy, but ask them a few questions, and you'll realize even they chose to redefine "having it all." If a woman is married with children and has a demanding career, she likely has a supportive husband and one or both of them have at times throttled back on their career commitments. Or she may have a nanny, parents, or in-laws who help with the children. If she is single, she may tell you she didn't mean to end up single in her 40s or 50s. One survey of women ages 41 to 55 who made over $100,000 per year showed that 49 percent had no children and only 14 percent of them intended to be single at this point in their lives.

So yes, we can have it all, but we often have to pay a price that men don't. Let's face it. Although the number of "stay-at-home dads" has tripled since the late 1990s, according the US Census Bureau, they still make up less than 3 percent of stay-home-parents. Successful men are simply more likely to have the support of a spouse willing to take on a traditional role that enables him to thrive at work without the demands of being the primary caregiver and household manager.

I am so grateful for those who came before us who fought for women's equality. We all deserve the opportunity to fulfill our potential using our gifts and talents, regardless of gender. Unlike our mothers and grandmothers before us, the question is no longer whether we have the ability to succeed in any given field of endeavor. We can succeed—and excel—whether in the marketplace or on the home front. The bigger question is this: Now that you can do *both*, now that you have so many choices that allow you to pursue pretty much anything you want in life…what is it that you really want? What will make you genuinely happy? And how can you design your life to embody true fulfillment and purpose? Dig deep for your unique answers. Our culture will offer you many opinions. Every woman's answer will differ. Get clear about your own.

Smile!

Why it's not just happy feelings that bring a smile, but why a smile (even a forced one) brings happy feelings

---

Decision

"Every day, I find a way to smile—*especially on bad days.*"

There was a man in a company I once worked for. He was one of the owners—very tall, salt-and-pepper gray with a thick mustache. I'll call him Jim. To me, a twenty-something young woman who smiled a lot, his presence coming down the hall could be a little intimidating. Normally, I found smiling to be contagious—I smile and the other person at least nods or turns up the corners of their mouth ever so slightly. But not Jim. His response was always a simple, monotone "Hi" with a straight face. No expression whatsoever.

Imagine my surprise one day when walking down the hall. As Jim walked toward me, he actually smiled *before* I did. I thought maybe someone was behind me and he was smiling at them, but no. It was just the two of us. I smiled back. "Something awfully good must have just happened to him," I thought. I'm not sure I'd ever really seen his teeth. They weren't bad! When he smiled, he looked nice. Although his smile did seem a little forced that day, it was such a nice departure from the poker-face, I welcomed it. A few days later, the same thing happened again. I was walking down the hallway and Jim smiled at me first.

After a third smiling encounter I mentioned it to a coworker, who laughed and admitted she was so perplexed when he did it to her that she asked his administrative assistant what was going on with Jim these days. Apparently, a 360-assessment had revealed his whole staff found him a bit of an intimidating figure—and as feedback from an outside consultant he was told to try smiling at people. Jim had told his admin, "It's working. People have been more talkative to me lately and seem a little more at ease." Soon, Jim's smile didn't seem forced at all. He seemed to genuinely enjoy his newfound interactions with people in the office.

> "A smile is a curve that sets everything
> straight." – *Phyllis Diller*

A smile, it turns out, can have a positive emotional impact—whether it's forced or real. It actually triggers the release of endorphins to your brain. Conventional wisdom is that happiness produces a smile, and this is certainly true. But smiling—or even just mimicking the physical attributes of a smile by doing something such as biting down on a pencil or saying a hard "Eee"—produces happy feelings. Obviously, having happy things happen that make you smile is preferable. However, the domino effect of smiling can actually lead you on the track to a happy place.

Once your brain "feels happy"—in other words, when it experiences a small bit of positive emotion—it can trigger you to think about positive things. Thinking about something good, whether it is something you are grateful for or noticing the opportunity in front of you to tackle the project you've been procrastinating on, can spark an upward spiral of positive emotion.

This really works. I've tried it in moments when, quite frankly, I was happy to wallow for a minute. Have you ever been there? You're feeling down. Something didn't go your way. You feel justified in moping and you are not in the mood to be jolted out of it. Look, moping holds a purpose. You get to feel sorry for yourself. You get to blame somebody. And you might even get some pity: *Poor thing. Of course we don't expect you to do anything. You just keep moping and pouting. You earned it.*

I've been in that pitiful place when I suddenly had the fleeting thought, "Why don't you jolt yourself out of this pity party and smile, just for kicks?" It is an odd thought in the midst of a bad mood, but intriguing nonetheless. And the part of me that's really milking the moping for all it's worth doesn't want to hear it! "Don't do it!" it begs, knowing that if I smile I'll feel better—even if only slightly. And if I feel any ounce of positive emotion, I'll want more. So, against the judgment of my inner pity party, I slowly turn up the corners of my mouth. I feel the endorphins releasing. I think about how silly I must look. I go to the mirror to see if I really look like I'm smiling. That leads to a full-on, toothy grin. Then I chuckle at myself. The few drops of positive emotion open my mind and I have a thought. "Besides sitting here and moping, what do I want to do about the situation? I'm resilient. I'm not going to let this defeat me. This feeling sorry for myself thing is getting kind of boring." At this point, the tide has begun to turn.

Even though your mind knows when you are pretend-smiling, your body doesn't. Why don't you try it with me now? It's a simple, little experiment in smiling.

1. Relax your face and turn the corners of your mouth upwards. Imagine you are creating a semicircle with your mouth.

2. Continue to expand the corners upward until you feel your cheeks getting bigger.

3. Continue until you feel your eyes crinkle a bit.

4. To really amp it up, expand your smile so that your pearly whites are showing. You may even feel the sensation that your eyes are lighting up. They are!

As silly as it may seem to simply make a decision to smile, do it anyway. Now, don't get me wrong. I'm not suggesting that if you have a major tragedy in your life, all you have to do is smile and everything will be fine. But I am saying that in those everyday moments, when your kids just spilled milk on the table for the third time this week or you just got cut off in traffic or your boss snapped at you *again* and now you feel like snapping at everybody in your path, try smiling.

Believe it or not, it happened to me just earlier this afternoon. I had to call my bank to activate my business credit card after asking my assistant to do it. Apparently they wouldn't allow her to, so when I called back they gave me a really hard time for having someone else call. I was in the middle of working, and frankly, it seems every time I turn around this bank is flagging my credit card for a fraud alert, which means when I go to make a purchase it gets inexplicably declined. "Well, Ms. Burton," the bank fraud rep says, "you were at a store in Minneapolis and we thought that was suspicious." Or, "Someone tried to use your credit card at a hotel in California, and we know you don't live anywhere near California so we decided to put a hold on your card until you call us and verify that that was indeed you in California." Every time I call, I say, "Yes! It was me! I travel for work! Can I please use my credit card now?" So today, when I called and the service person's tone suggested I might have been calling fraudulently, my stress level spiked. Her attitude seemed to be one of annoyance rather than helpfulness, as though I had bothered her afternoon nap rather than dialing a call center where she was presumably waiting to answer calls just like mine.

Have you ever been in this kind of situation? Before I knew it, I was asking for a supervisor. (Yes! I, the happy woman, got jolted out of a perfectly happy mood by a stranger on the phone!) By the time I hung up, I was stressed. Flushed with frustration from the call, I had to intentionally shift my mood. I stopped. I clasped my hands together and rested my chin on them. I took a few deep breaths. I closed my eyes and slowly, I smiled. Breathe. Smile. Hold. Breathe. Smile. Hold. "Lord," I said. "I can't let silly stuff get to me. Thank you that I have a whole lot to be happy about."

It's a simple formula: Breathe. Smile. Pray. It works.

Here are the benefits of smiling, even on a day when you feel like you don't want to smile:

- Smiling automatically moves you from a place of thinking to a place of feeling. It helps you get outside your head and inside your own heart.

- A smile triggers the release of serotonin, a calming hormone, as well as endorphins. These hormones help you relax and improve how you feel. The ensuing positive emotions actually expand your ability to think more clearly.

- Smiling fights negative thoughts. Try this. Go ahead and smile right now. Go ahead. You smiling? Make sure you are smiling before you read the next sentence. Okay. Now, while you continue to smile, I want you to visualize a situation that feels negative to you. It is very hard to do, isn't it?

- Smiling can change the atmosphere. You can change the entire mood in a room by smiling. A smile is universal. If you have ever been to a foreign country or attempted to talk to someone whose language is different from your own, you know that in every language, a smile communicates approachable, warm, and happy.

- A smile connects people. Because smiling is contagious and moves you from your head to your heart, it is a powerful tool for connecting with people. It says, "I welcome you into my space."

A Confident Smile Means Smiling More Often

Negative feelings aren't the only thing that can keep you from smiling. If you don't feel good about how your smile looks, you are less likely to smile. I've known many women over the years who intentionally avoid showing their teeth because they don't like what they see when they do. If that's you, why not make it a goal to do something about it? In my observation, there is no better cosmetic improvement than improving your smile. Whether it's getting braces or whitening your teeth because time has left them stained or yellowing, it is one of the few cosmetic changes that can actually increase happiness by giving you more confidence to flash your pearly whites.

Over the years I've had several opportunities to partner with companies whose products and values mirror my own, but one opportunity that really resonated with me was Crest toothpaste. They first approached me in 2012 for a campaign with BET and Black Girls

Rock, and now I am a part of the Crest SHINE Network. It's easy for me to partner with a company that brightens smiles because when you feel confident that your smile looks good, you're more likely to actually do more smiling! And more smiling means more happy feelings.

The Duchenne Smile

There's more to smiles that make your eyes crinkle than just releasing healthy hormones into your body that lift your mood. A smile that engages the muscles around your mouth and eyes is called a Duchenne smile, named after French physician Guillaume Duchenne. In the mid-nineteenth century Dr. Duchenne identified two types of smiles: the kind that raises your cheeks, creating little crow's feet around your eyes, and what was later dubbed the Pan-Am smile, named for the now-defunct airline whose flight attendants always gave each passenger a polite smile as they boarded the plane. The Pan-Am smile only engages the zygomatic major muscle, which raises the corners of your mouth.

In a 2001 study, researchers analyzed 114 photographs of young women at a women's college in the San Francisco Bay area.[1] The pictures were from the 1958 and 1960 yearbooks. There were only three women in the photos who did not smile at all, but of the 111 who smiled, some showed a Duchenne smile while others flashed the Pan-Am smile. The smiles were rated on a ten-point scale for "Duchenneness," and the average smile received a 3.8 rating. The researchers also rated the photos for attractiveness. In other words, totally separate from the smile, how attractive was the subject of each picture? The significance of choosing these particular photos was important, because the women photographed were also a part of a longitudinal study. The researchers had information about whether the women were married and just how happy they were in their marriages. Interestingly, the women with Duchenne smiles were more likely to get married and to be happier in their marriages decades later. Attractiveness, however, did not predict who was happy in their marriage.

Duchenne smiles are genuine, and therefore, tend to indicate the presence of positive emotions. We know from research that positive emotions have a positive impact on health, longevity, and relationships, and this study is an interesting support of that. From a spiritual perspective, I think of Nehemiah 8:10, which states, "The joy of the LORD is your strength." Joy, indeed, strengthens us in numerous ways. But the women's college study isn't the only one that points to positive correlations between Duchenne smiles and positive outcomes later in life.

A 2010 study of player photographs from the 1952 Major League Baseball season yielded equally intriguing results.[2] The study analyzed photos of 150 players who, by June of 2009, were deceased. Players who didn't smile in the pictures had an average life span of 72 years. Those who gave a Pan-Am smile lived about 75 years on average. But those who had genuine Duchenne smiles lived for 80 years! A genuine smile is worth years of life.

Women Show and Read Facial Expression More than Men

Women tend to show their emotions on their faces more than men, and research shows we are also more adept at reading emotional expressions than men. It is possible then that as a woman, you are more influenced by a smiling face than your male counterparts. Could that explain why Jim's persistent poker-face made me feel so uncomfortable each time I smiled at him as we passed in the hallway? Maybe.

An article in *Scientific American* pointed to research at the University of Cardiff in Wales that studied women who were injected with Botox that inhibited their ability to frown.[3] The results showed that those unable to frown reported feeling happier and less anxious. Interestingly, they did not report feeling any more attractive than the women who did not receive Botox injections, so researchers concluded that the happy feelings could not be attributed to giddiness about having fewer wrinkles. "It would appear that the way we feel emotions isn't just restricted to our brain—there are parts of our bodies that help and reinforce the feelings we're having," noted the study's coauthor, Michael Lewis, in the article. "It's like a feedback loop."

Negative feelings don't just bring a frown, but the frown brings additional negative feelings. Without the ability to frown, the negative feelings are less intense. Another study, published in the *Journal of Pain*, showed that those who make unhappy faces while experiencing pain report feeling higher levels of pain than those who relax their faces while experiencing pain. Again, the facial expression intensifies the feeling. These findings mirror the physiological response of a smile. Happy feelings don't just bring a smile to your face. A smile on your face brings happy feelings. There is a feedback loop between your face and your feelings.

To be clear, you should not avoid frowning when you are sad in order to thwart negative feelings on a regular basis. Research shows that if you suppress your negative emotions altogether, they will eventually emerge in other ways.

Even though science proves that smiling—whether genuine or not—can bring happy feelings, it is much better when you can actually have a real reason to smile. Sometimes this means taking yourself less seriously. Finding a way to laugh at yourself—or just laugh *period*—is a sure way to a genuine smile.

Just for Laughs

"A cheerful heart is good medicine, but a crushed spirit dries up the bones" (Proverbs 17:22).

If you were ever a *Seinfeld* fan, perhaps you remember the episode in which Jerry dates a woman and his friends point out to him that she never laughs. Instead, when Jerry says something funny, she just replies in a deadpan tone, "That's funny." It's quite ironic since she's dating a comedian. And it brings me to this point: Laughter is not meant to be held in, controlled, watered down.

LOL is so overused today that no one really means it when they write it! But it's time for you to LOL. Literally. Every day, something ought to make you laugh out loud. So open your mouth. Smile big. Laugh out loud—from your belly. No closed-mouthed laughing allowed—it sounds ridiculous and makes you look constipated. I once knew a woman who always laughed with her mouth closed, like she was going to get into trouble if she really let it out. She pressed her lips together and made a little giggle noise from her throat. Sometimes, when it became way too hard for her to keep it in, the laughter would push its way out through her nose, like bad snoring on the exhale.

One day I said, "How come you laugh so quietly?"

She laughed (with her mouth closed) at my question, and then said, "I hadn't thought about it. Is that what I do?"

"Yes! And I just want you to let it out!" I replied.

"You know, when I was a kid, I got in trouble for laughing and a relative told me it wasn't ladylike for girls to laugh loudly, so I came up with a cute laugh that wasn't so loud," she reflected.

"Do you still believe that?" I asked.

"Well, actually, no," she said.

Laughing is healthy. And as adults, we don't do enough of it. If you have trouble laughing, spend some time around babies. The average baby laughs 300 times a day. The average adult? Just 20 times a day. Like smiling, laughter is a universal human language. Neurophysiologists explain that laughter activates the ventromedial prefrontal cortex, a part of the brain that produces endorphins. Laughter has been shown to reduce the stress hormones cortisol and epinephrine. It can actually boost your immune system—and your brain power. The resulting positive emotions expand your ability to learn and absorb new information. This is why speakers often start with a joke and do well to incorporate humor into their presentations, no matter how serious the subject matter. So just how can you incorporate more laughter into your day. Consider these ideas:

- Lighten up and laugh at yourself!
- Spend time around people who laugh.
- Watch something funny.
- Play with a baby or young children.
- Tell and listen to humorous stories and memories.

I feel blessed to come from a family that laughs. On his way into corrective open heart surgery, as I stood at his bedside and the nurses came to wheel him away, my dad was cracking jokes. I was a bit anxious, but him? Nope. "God didn't bring me this far to take me now!" he said. He was actually smiling as he was whisked off. My parents, cousins, aunts, uncles, *everybody* laughs. Maybe that's one of the reasons we are so close. We get together for family reunions every summer. I've never known of anyone to quit talking to somebody, even when they are not pleased with something they did. And we are mushy. "I love you" flies around like "hello" in my family. We've been through some very difficult life events, some of them traumatic, but we remain connected. I'm never happier than when I'm with my family.

Sitting around reminiscing about funny stories one evening with my Auntie Margaret and Uncle Bobby, my dad told a story that illustrates the true power of laughter and its meaning in life. My father remembered how in the last few minutes of his father's life, my granddaddy was laughing and smiling. He looked at my dad just minutes before he drew his last breath and said with a smile, "Junior, don't let the big bird get ya!"

Granddaddy was referring to a moment that had occurred more than two decades earlier when my father was just nine years old. It was the early 1960s, long before school shootings made adults more leery of exposing children to guns. Granddaddy was a hunter and told my dad, "It's time for me to get you your own shotgun so you can learn how to hunt." They went to the store, purchased a shotgun, and early one Saturday morning, with sack lunches of bologna sandwiches and soda in hand, they drove out to the woods with the dogs to hunt.

"We left around 6:30 a.m. and by dusk, I was exhausted," my dad recalls. "We had been in the woods all day. I think Daddy was starting to get a little aggravated with me too. I really wasn't much for hunting and I was getting tired, so he decided to let me rest while he finished his last bit of hunting before dark."

"Sit right here," Granddaddy said. "I'll be back in a little bit. Holler if you need me!"

My dad sat quietly under a tree and laid his brand new shotgun on the ground next to him. He could hear Granddaddy and the dogs in the distance. But it was another sound that left room for pause. "I heard a low, deep shushing noise. Almost like a vibration, but I'd never heard it before so I couldn't really distinguish quite what it was. I was sure, though, that the noise was being made by some kind of animal. And it sounded like it was coming from above my head."

That's when he remembered something Granddaddy had told him one Sunday when they were coming home from church and saw an eagle flying alongside the road with the biggest wingspan he'd ever seen. Granddaddy had told him, "Son, an eagle has claws so big he could pick up a sixty-pound boy like you and carry him off like it was nothing!"

Now, in this moment, those words rang in his ears. "What if that sound is coming from an eagle?" he thought. Right then, little Johnny Burton looked up and saw a massive bird sitting on a branch just above him with large, round eyes and a head as big as his own. The bird was looking straight at him. And to his shock and terror, the bird's head did a complete 360 degree turn! Johnny didn't want to give the horrifying eagle a chance to get him, so he took off running as fast as he could, screaming as he went.

"Daddy! Daddy!" he yelled as he ran through the woods, sure the big-headed eagle was close behind him, preparing his claws to grab little Johnny by the shirt.

He didn't know where exactly his father was, but his father could hear him. He ran frantically. The dogs barked in the distance. And Granddaddy yelled instructions to his little boy, having no idea what danger his son was in. "Junior?" Granddaddy yelled to his son. "I'm coming, Junior! Run to the open field! I'll meet you in the open field!"

Johnny ran and ran, and after what felt like an eternity he made it to the open field. Seeing that his son was all right, Granddaddy asked, "What's wrong, son? What happened?"

Out of breath and panting hard, little Johnny explained the horror. "A big bird! A big bird!" he said excitedly. "A big bird was coming after me!" he managed to say between gasps for breath.

Perplexed, Granddaddy looked around. There was no bird in sight.

"Why didn't you shoot the bird?" he asked, perplexed. Then he noticed his son didn't have his shotgun. "Boy, where's your gun?" he asked.

Speechless, Johnny looked at his hands. He'd left his shotgun on the ground under the tree. To make matters even more comical, there was clearly no bird coming after him.

They stood there in the middle of the field laughing uncontrollably.

"Let's go find your gun. And this big bird," Granddaddy said. They walked back to the tree and sure enough, the shotgun was on the ground. The bird was still sitting on the same branch. It had not moved an inch. And it wasn't an eagle. It was an owl.

Lying on his death bed in the last few minutes of his life, Granddaddy recalled this story. It made him smile. In the last moments of his life, he laughed reminiscing about a funny moment with his son two decades earlier.

It confirms for me the power of everything that brings happiness—relationships, play, laughter, connection, and savoring.

Activate This Happiness Trigger!

- Turn up the corners of your mouth until those cheeks puff and your eyes crinkle. Ahh…

- When you feel happy feelings, let it show on your face! Express yourself.

- Laugh—not a little, but a lot!

Taming Your Expectations

*How the "Queen of Happy" Lost Her
Happy and Found It Again*

- What expectations stress you out?
- What pressures leave you feeling as though you are not doing enough or being enough?
- What expectations do you try to live up to that are not necessarily what God has asked you to do?

As genuinely excited as I was to write a book on happiness, I didn't realize how intimidating a subject it could be to write about. After all, writing a book kind of indicates you might be an expert on the subject. And being an expert on the subject of happiness might just indicate that you have it all figured it out—the poster child for a happy woman. Granted, some of the people in my life would say that's about right. In fact, I recall an interview on CNN a couple of years ago in which the anchor, upon introducing me, called me the "Queen of Happy!" Catchy title, but my goodness, that's a lot of pressure.

Then I decided to write a book on the subject! I didn't anticipate it, but the anxiety started to pile on. "Will writing this book mean I can never be unhappy?" I asked myself. "Am I committing myself to a permanent smile every time I step out of the door? Am I no longer allowed to have a bad day?" As I dove into this project, these were the questions I encountered—not loud and scary, but soft whispers hovering just above the surface of my consciousness, reminding me gently but persistently of the times in my life when I was *not* happy, of the moments I forgot to be grateful, fell into pessimism, or lost my patience with someone after a long, exhausting week. *Can you live up to the expectation of this book?*, the thoughts probed. *Are you smart enough? Happy enough? Expert enough?* As I resisted the thoughts, they became stronger and my writing weaker, until midway through the project eventually my frustration drove me to my knees in prayer.

Lord, writing a book about being happy should not *make me unhappy. What on earth is going on with me? Are you trying to send me a message? Because usually when I get frustrated and stuck, it means you're trying to get my attention. Well, you have my attention! What do you want for this book? What do you want to say? I need you to write through me, or this is probably not going to get written. And that would make me really sad because I believe it is meant to be. But nothing I write will matter unless it's what you want women to know. So I surrender my worries and anxieties to you. If it's going to get done, it will be because you gave me the strength, the courage, and the wisdom. I'm all ears. Amen.*

Almost immediately, I felt a release. He spoke. Here's what I sensed in my spirit:

I didn't put all this pressure on you, Valorie—to write perfectly, to make it big and complicated. That's you. Remember this: My burden is light and my yoke is easy! If that's not how this is feeling to you, then it's not from me. My expectations of you are to write from your heart. Share what you've learned. Raise awareness about the changing culture that's making it increasingly harder for women to be happy unless they are very intentional about it. And my goodness, have fun! Writing is what I created you for, so be happy.

One of the biggest lessons about women and happiness is this: Sky-high expectations *steal* your happiness. Trying to live up to what everyone else thinks and wants for you is a recipe for perpetual anxiety, self-doubt, and a generally unhappy life. So if you find yourself asking the "enough" questions, let me just answer them for you right now. Yes! You are enough for whatever it is you are meant to be doing in your life. As women in today's culture, we too often have looming self-doubt about whether we are doing enough or being enough at work, at home, in church, and with our children. The doors that were not open to our mothers and grandmothers—the doors they worked tirelessly to open for us—have led down the road to plenty of opportunity and, unexpectedly, plenty of worry.

Now that we've begun this journey together on the road to a happier version of you, I want to let you in on something: I am happy. But I do not claim to be an *expert*. Instead, I prefer to call myself a *student* of happiness. That's a title that fits me well, lets me breathe, and makes me smile. I am on a journey to explore answers and then share what I find, spark fruitful conversation, illuminate cultural shifts, and inspire personal change. That's who I am. When I took an assessment to discover my signature strengths, it was no surprise that among my top five is "love of learning." It intrigues me to study what makes us happy and what doesn't. It bothers me to know that over the last four decades, women's happiness has begun to decline while men, for some reason, continue to get happier. Not because I don't want the men to be happy, but because I'm deeply curious and eager to answer this question: *What is going on with us?*

In fact, this is the question that got me started down this path. I began asking friends, colleagues, strangers on airplanes—Why do you think women get sadder as they get older and men don't? Is your life what you thought it would be or are you disappointed in some way? Do you have it all? Have you *tried* to have it all? How's that working out for you? And not once did a woman answer, "I don't know." They all had an opinion!

Most expressed frustration. Many mentioned not being able to live up to expectations. Others—many others—talked about feeling guilty. Guilty about not being a better mother or wife. Guilty about not always giving their all at work. Guilty that in attempting to do it all, they've discovered it is pretty hard to do it all really well. "When will I ever have done enough?" they asked. "There is always something left to do, something more to pursue."

It seems that one of the keys is finding a balance between optimism and realism, shooting for the stars (if you want to) while simultaneously keeping your feet firmly planted on earth, able to enjoy simple but profound pleasures. Give yourself permission to be human and appreciate the ordinary.

Service

*How individualism is ruining your happiness and
why you should embrace your urge to nurture*

Decision

"Every day, I do at least one thing to brighten someone else's day."

One of the most profound spiritual lessons of all time is described in John 13 as Jesus washes the disciples' feet before the Last Supper. It was the act of a servant, seemingly beneath Jesus. Peter even protested, saying, "No. You shall never wash my feet" (John 13:8). But Jesus explained that unless he washed his feet, Peter would have no part with him.

> "Do you understand what I have done for you?" he asked them. "You call me 'Teacher' and 'Lord,' and rightly so, for that is what I am. Now that I, your Lord and Teacher, have washed your feet, you also should wash one another's feet. I have set you an example that you should do as I have done for you" (John 13:12-15).

He summed up the concept of service in Matthew 23:11 when he said, "The greatest among you will be your servant."

It could also be said that the happiest among us are servants. When you are constantly focused on what you can get, anxiety and greed threaten to consume you. However, when your focus is on what you are meant to give in any given situation, there is no anxiety. Showing up to serve produces no anxiety, but it does produce peace and joy. Every day, you must ask yourself, "Who can I bless today? Who am I meant to serve?" Sometimes those blessings will be small—an encouraging word to a coworker who needs it or picking up after your hubby even though you wish he'd quit leaving his shoes and socks in the middle of the living room when he comes home. Other times, you will feel called to serve and give in a more substantial way.

Beth had just received a job transfer from California to Michigan. In addition to an apartment full of furniture to pack up, she would need to get her two cars to Michigan as well. Her brother volunteered to help her drive to the Midwest, but the other car would need to be shipped. She'd had it since college (and it was already a few years old when she got it), so it was now ten years old with just over 100,000 miles on it. But it was a Volkswagen, so she knew it had a lot more life left, and she didn't want to part with it. It would last several more years and make a great car to drive in all that Michigan snow. All she'd ever had to do was get oil changes, tune-ups, and new tires. It would be worth paying a car shipping service to haul the car to her new city. But one morning as Beth brushed her teeth, a random thought entered her mind: "Give the car to Sylvia."

"What?" she thought as she continued to brush vigorously.

Sylvia was a young woman at church who was raising a little girl and boy on her own. Beth's friend Lisa had mentioned that Sylvia couldn't take a better paying job on the other side of town because her car kept breaking down and she couldn't afford a new one, and didn't want to take on a job when she knew she didn't have reliable transportation.

Beth stopped brushing and stood in front of the mirror. Tears began to stream down her face. She had never struggled to have reliable transportation. As a teenager and college student, her parents had given her a car. She had a good job as an accountant right out of college. For two years now, she'd had two cars—the one from college had been paid for for many years. She realized in that moment just how blessed she was and had an overwhelming urge to bless Sylvia.

She called Lisa to find out how to get in touch with her. It was a Saturday. She called Sylvia and asked if they could chat after the church service the next day. When she saw her in person, she gave her the news—she wanted to bless her with a car, no strings attached. Sylvia was speechless at first. Then she began to cry. "You have no idea," she said in an emotional whisper. "I just sat here and prayed for God to help me in some kind of way. I told him, I want to do better, but I need transportation that's reliable! And here, thirty minutes after my prayer, you tell me this!" Sylvia thanked Beth profusely. She told the kids and they started jumping up and down.

Beth felt like she was on cloud nine. Something that she'd taken for granted, and didn't cost her anything to do, had made a huge difference in the life of this family.

There are ways you could make a difference for someone, just like Sylvia. The sacrifice would be minimal to you but monumental to the other person. You have knowledge to share that others are in the dark about. Do you mentor anyone with that knowledge? You have possessions you haven't used or wouldn't miss if you gave away, but those possessions would mean the world to someone who doesn't have them. Are you hoarding your stuff or looking for ways to bless others with it? You have a smile that would brighten anyone's day, but for some reason you look serious everywhere you go. Could you lighten up and spread some sunshine? You never know what the people around you are going through. Serve them good cheer and kindness.

Among effective leaders, the most common character strength, surprisingly, is not "leadership" or "bravery and valor," but the "capacity to love and be loved." Why? One reason is likely that when people feel you care about them, they are more likely to trust and follow you and do anything to help you succeed. At the core of serving others is love. You cannot love without serving. You cannot serve without love. They are inextricably intertwined—not only with each other, but with your personal happiness.

Made to Serve

We were created to serve. The core of your purpose in life is serving, but service is not just about life purpose. It is about simple ways we can positively impact others throughout any given day. If you are going to be happy, then every day, find a way to brighten someone else's day. Plain and simple. Take the focus off yourself and place it on someone else.

Have you ever just gotten tired thinking about the problems you're trying to solve? It is exhausting thinking about yourself constantly. *Will I get that raise? Will I lose this weight? Will I get married? Will I get the promotion? Will I get to stop working and stay home? How does my hair look? What did she say about me?* See a theme here? Thinking about "me, me, me" is a sure recipe for unhappiness. And a quick way to turn it around is to put your mind on somebody else. Did you know someone needs you right now? Somebody needs your smile. Someone needs your encouragement. Somebody would absolutely give anything to live the life you are living right now. They would love to hear how you succeeded at that thing you succeeded at. But they'll never hear that unless you take the time to direct your energy toward them.

It has been said that the ultimate pessimism is depression. An inward focus on yourself and all that is wrong in your life is pessimism. The individualism that has become prevalent in the last 60 years erodes our commitment to others, Dr. Martin Seligman noted in his research. "People born after 1945 were 10 times more likely to suffer depression than those born 50 years earlier."[1] I'll never forget the Christmas many, many years ago when plans unfolded that left me alone on Christmas Day. I was in my mid-twenties and single and no member of my family was going to be in town on Christmas. I started my pity party. "I don't have a boyfriend, let alone a husband. Nobody's thinking about me. I guess I'll just sit around and open presents by myself. Maybe I should even go buy some things for myself and wrap them up so I have more gifts to open. How pitiful is that? Buying my own presents and wrapping them?" Oh, I was pitiful all right. I love Joyce Meyer's saying: "You can be pitiful or powerful, but you can't be both." It certainly applied to me.

I was rehashing my pitiful story to a good friend about a week before Christmas and she said, "Why don't you come with us to give out gifts and serve meals on Christmas Day?" She and her boyfriend had decided to serve on the holiday.

"That sounds fun," I told her. "If you don't mind me tagging along."

So the three of us arrived at an old theater on Christmas morning with a few gifts of food items of our own in tow. The nonprofit that organized the day trained and instructed us on how the day would unfold and what we needed to do. Within a couple of hours, parents began arriving on buses that had been chartered to pick them up and bring them with their children to the theater. Each family received a hot Christmas dinner and groceries to carry home and we personally handed gifts to the children. Can I tell you they were genuinely excited? They were thankful. They were humble. They put the "woe is me" attitude I'd had all season to shame. And that was exactly what I needed: perspective. That day was one of the happiest Christmases I ever had. Rather than getting, I gave. Serving made me happy. It made me grateful. It reminded me of what we are all here for—to serve one another.

9 Ways to Serve Somebody Today

1. Ask the question.

Three self-coaching questions will get your day started on a happy note. When you wake up in the morning, first ask, "Who will I bless today?" Second, ask, "What am I looking forward to?" Third, ask, "What am I most grateful for?" You'll activate the happiness triggers of service, anticipation, and gratitude in the first five minutes after you wake up!

2. Hold the door.

Service is practical. It is doing something for the benefit of another person. In a world in which we are often faced with rudeness and disconnection, intentionally commit random acts of kindness, such as holding the door for that person you see with your peripheral vision. You know they are behind you. Don't pretend they aren't there!

3. Give grace.

"There but for the grace of God go I." It's not all about you. I know that thing you need is taking longer than you'd like, but it will get done, even if it doesn't get done in your timing. How about choosing to be patient and giving that person the grace to make mistakes? Grace takes humility. Servants are humble. They give others the grace to be human.

4. Give your loved ones what they want, not what you want.

Without realizing it, we often give others the love we want them to give us. But giving what you want makes your act of love about you, not them. Yes, you might like getting flowers and gifts, but your hubby would rather you stop what you're doing and spend the afternoon lying on the sofa with him watching the football game. That would make him happy.

5. Volunteer to help.

The simplest way to serve is to find a need and help fill it. Are you active with a nonprofit organization or ministry that makes a difference in your community or around the world?

6. Adopt a family.

If you have the means or experience to help someone who is struggling to make ends meet or could use some guidance to strengthen their family, why not make it your mission to help them? Perhaps the person didn't have anyone to model for them what good parenting looks like. Or they need help learning to make better financial decisions. Or you see potential that is untapped and you might just be the encourager who inspires them to do something more with themselves.

7. Mentor a young woman.

Whether through a formal program such as Big Brothers Big Sisters or informally through your church, family, or neighborhood connections, invest in the life of a girl or young woman by taking an interest in helping her lay a strong foundation to lead a purposeful, happy life.

8. Smile.

This is easy. Spread sunshine wherever you go. Be friendly. Smile. It's contagious. Soon, you'll create a domino effect. What a simple way to serve the world around you.

9. Listen.

Few people get the opportunity to truly feel heard. You can be that person who listens. Sometimes, all someone needs is a listening ear. You will hear it in their appreciation.

Serving Your Family

It is easy to think of service as solely what we do "out there" in the world where there are so many people in need. But it is also what we do in our closest relationships. If love and service are interchangeable, how are you when it comes to serving your family? Are you generous or do you withhold? What matters to your spouse? Your children? Your parents? Real love must first be expressed in the home.

Ask yourself these self-coaching questions.

- If you are honest with yourself, do you focus more on serving or being served?

- What have you done recently to help someone in need?

- In what ways could you better serve others?

- In what way(s) might your life be too much about you and not enough about others?

- What gets in the way of you serving? What could you do about that?

Activate This Happiness Trigger!

- Take the focus off of yourself today. Focus your energy on a random act of service.

- Do an inventory of your possessions—clothes, computers, household items, everything. Out of your abundance, what could you bless someone with?

- Make a list of people in your life you'd like to bless, including your spouse and family members.

Is It Okay That I Don't Want to Conquer the World?

*What used to be the norm is now the stigma
of being professionally unambitious*

Points to Ponder:

- Women in past generations had fewer options, but also fewer roles they were expected to fill.

- Ambition can apply to areas of life other than a career.

- Among college-educated Generation X women, 43 percent did not have any children by 2011.

Conversation starters:

- Is it acceptable to be decidedly unambitious in your professional life?

- What expectations were placed on you out of high school or college? Were they aligned with what you wanted for yourself?

- Why do you think so many professional women today are stepping out of the workforce? What feelings do they wrestle with?

- What is the point of earning a law or graduate degree (or even a bachelor's degree) if you are not going to work?

"When I finished high school, there was no expectation that I would go conquer the world," 60-year-old Lynn explained matter-of-factly. She graduated high school, married two years later, and had a baby. In her own words, she could not have been happier—seriously. "I absolutely loved everything about being a mom and having a little baby to take care of. She was like a real-life doll to me," she reminisces. "My husband was early in his career and didn't make much, but that really didn't matter. We had everything we needed, plus good friends and a healthy baby."

Dara is a little younger, in her late forties with four children. She finished college with a degree in economics, but never had a desire to use her degree. "I went to college to get an education, but all I ever wanted was to be a wife and a mom," she says. "And even now, that still makes me happy. I don't feel like I missed out on anything. For me, having it all is being a wife and a mom. Being in the business world was never a part of the equation."

Andrea's story is different from Lynn and Dara's, but with a similar theme. In her early forties and married with no children, she is smart, insightful, happy—and decidedly unambitious. "I've never been ambitious. I don't sit around thinking about my goals," she admits.

Now honestly, the first time she said this, I was perplexed. I frowned at the thought. "You don't think about your goals? It doesn't bother you to be unambitious?" I wondered suspiciously. "Maybe she just isn't tuned in to her heart's desires," I rationalized. But I was intrigued. Happily married, she loves life. She works as a volunteer and is actively involved in her niece's and nephew's lives—sometimes helping shuttle them to basketball and ballet practice. She's not stressed. And she's happy with where she is in life. She's not trying to force herself to become more ambitious.

The more I listened to Andrea, watching her talk in her own genuine way, I realized this is just who she is. Not every woman derives deep happiness and contentment from achievement.

"I don't want to conquer the world," she says. "I just don't."

It is a powerful statement. And in today's success-driven culture that defines success largely by professional and financial accomplishments, it is almost politically incorrect for a woman to say, "Hey! That's not what I want to do." But what if, like Andrea, you're not interested in achievement? Is it okay to want less instead of more when it comes to your career?

It is a matter of personal choice. You've got to understand your purpose and allow a vision for your life to emerge based on that purpose. God didn't wire us all the same way. Some are more driven than others. And some are driven, but it's not a professional drive for a business or a 9-to-5.

Lower Expectations, More Happiness

Now, you know I want you to reach your highest potential. So I would never tell you to lower your sights. In fact, I think it is critical not to downsize your dreams. *The dreams that God has placed in your heart are for you.* You really cannot fail at what the Creator created you to do. But not all dreams are God-given dreams. Some dreams are expectations we've placed on ourselves that add pressure and stress that is entirely unnecessary. Some dreams are expectations others have placed on us that add pressure and stress—and we can allow fear of disapproval to drive us toward dreams that aren't even our own. In what way(s) have you done that?

Each woman I interviewed whose expectations or definition of "having it all" was less than the generally accepted definition of having it all said she was happy. The only exceptions were women who struggled with comparing themselves with others—not just with other women, but even their own husbands.

In preparation for a college reunion program in which each couples' accomplishments would be highlighted, Ellen was deeply bothered that she could not list any professional accomplishments to include in the program while her husband had to edit his list just to make it fit on the page! "What have I done all these years?" she questioned herself. "What am I going to talk about? My kids are grown and married. They've got their own lives. What do I have?" Now, from the outside, Ellen's conclusion seemed rather harsh. She'd raised three productive, kind, spiritually-grounded, loving children. She had supported her husband, brought her extended family together, and lived an incredibly blessed life. In fact, it was precisely the life she'd hoped for. She got what she wanted. But being asked to describe the last 25 years of her life in terms of professional accomplishments hit a nerve.

There is danger in "comparing up." It can become a trigger for unhappiness, and that is precisely what happened to Ellen. You could be perfectly happy with your decision not to work, or to work but not climb the corporate ladder or build the big business. But if you begin comparing yourself with others who are more professionally ambitious, you will begin to doubt yourself. Comparing up will always leave you feeling less happy. The key to healthy comparison is to make sure it is balanced. You might notice what those who are more ambitious manage to accomplish professionally, but also make sure to notice the accomplishments of those who are *less* ambitious. Then, and most importantly, acknowledge and celebrate the blessing of your own accomplishments.

Financial Savvy

*Learn to avoid money choices that sabotage your
happiness and make choices that boost it*

Decision

"I aim to live on less than 75 percent of my income."

"Mo' Money, Mo' Problems!" That's what the late Biggie Smalls lamented in his 1990s rap anthem, but alas, Biggie was wrong. The truth is, money can make you happier. I know. It doesn't sound spiritual. It may sound materialistic. It's not. Hear me out. If you learn how to spend your money in the right ways, *money can trigger your personal happiness.*

This helps explain why among the ranking of the happiest nations in the world, the wealthiest nations top the list. None of the world's poorest countries are among the happiest countries. Nations where the people are poor and the governments oppressive have the least happy people in the world. When your basic needs aren't met, you don't worry about figuring out how happy women live better. Happiness is not a priority. Survival is.

In wealthy nations, in nearly every study, rich people report higher levels of happiness than those with poor or average incomes. Listen, money makes people measurably happier—especially if you don't have much to begin with and you experience a boost in income. Research shows that increases in happiness based on income are sharpest among those who have very little. If you live below the poverty line and get an income boost that catapults you into the middle class, you will be dramatically happier! With your newfound income, you can find somewhere safe to live. You can buy healthier food, and enough of it. If you live below your means, you can pay your bills. If you can pay your bills, the bill collectors aren't hounding you. Yes, you will be much, much happier.

After a household income of about $75,000, increases in happiness based solely on income are not that dramatic. But they still exist. Money gives you options. When used well, it empowers you to help others. It allows you to create experiences you might not otherwise be able to afford—a trip to see family during the holidays or concert tickets to see your favorite performer with your sweetheart, for example.

> "He who is not contented with what he
> has, would not be contented with what
> he would like to have." – *Socrates*

The key to triggering your happiness doesn't lie in the money itself. The key is in how you spend it. There are some simple steps you can take starting today to use your money to be happier. I'll share ten of them shortly. But first, let's talk about the flip side.

There are few things more stressful than not being able to pay your bills, living paycheck to paycheck, or fighting with your spouse about money. From a spiritual perspective, the fact that scripture says "the love of money is the root of all evil" causes many to shy away from suggesting that money can make you happy. So let me be clear. The *love of money* is the root of all sorts of horrible social ills, from greed and crime to cheating and gold-digging. But money itself? Money, when managed well, is a tool for doing good and living well. And if you learn to build wealth and become an excellent steward of it, you will be happier. If instead, you build debt and use your money to accumulate material things for the purpose of feeling better, happier, or more valuable, you'll fail miserably and continually wonder why you aren't a happier woman.

Emotionally, as women, we experience higher highs and lower lows than men. Negative emotional issues in particular can influence how you handle your money. So first I want to talk about emotional spending, and then I'll share ten specific ways money can make you happier.

Emotional Spending = Emotionally Draining

Emotional spending is both a symptom and a cause of unhappiness. Emotional spending occurs when you are motivated to spend money to consciously or unconsciously fill a void left by sadness, heartache, boredom, resentment, anger, anxiety, or any other negative emotion you seek to numb. Similar to emotional eating, instead of racking up pounds, you rack up credit card debt and drain your bank account. It becomes a vicious cycle because the more you spend emotionally, the more unhappy you become with yourself for your lack of self-control and tendency to sabotage your own financial security.

Consider this story.

I was standing in the lavish dressing room of a posh department store years ago waiting for a friend I'll call Tina to come out. It wouldn't have seemed so perplexing except she'd just told me over lunch that she'd been laid off. Then she promptly suggested we walk over to Neiman Marcus to find her a pantsuit for an upcoming job interview. She emerged from the dressing room, stunning in the black Armani suit as the sales associate fussed over her and brought in the seamstress to tailor it perfectly. She soaked up the attention.

"Are you sure you want to spend this kind of money right now?" I asked. "You have a lot of fabulous suits already."

"I need something new," she insisted. "I love this suit. I feel so confident in it!"

With that, Tina plunked down her store credit card—and its 22.5 percent interest rate—to spend nearly $3,000 that day on one outfit. If Tina could have afforded to pay cash for the purchase, wasn't already saddled with close to six figures of student loan debt, and had an income, this story wouldn't be worth telling. But she didn't. Tina was depressed and lonely at the time. And spending money at expensive stores, wearing the most coveted brand names, and being seen driving her luxury vehicle fed her craving for attention and her need to feel valuable.

We all have different ways of coping with insecurities, and too many of us have coped through emotional spending.

Now, your spending might not be as extreme as Tina's—or hey, it might be worse. Not sure you fit the profile? See if any of these statements describe your behavior:

- You sometimes buy things because you feel you deserve them, even if you can't afford them.

- You buy high-status brands because you want others to see that you are "successful."

- You go shopping when you feel sad, lonely, bored, deprived, or frustrated.

- You get an emotional high when you plunk down that credit card to make a purchase. In that moment, you feel powerful and in control.

- You purchase things for your children out of guilt that their other parent isn't around or that you work too much and don't spend enough time with them.

If you see yourself in any of these statements, listen up: Emotional spending is a reaction—a behavior you have the power to change. In my book *What's Really Holding You Back?*, I talk about allowing your emotions to school you rather than rule you. That's exactly what I want you to do. Here's how:

1. Add up your debt. If you support your habit with credit cards and loans, add up how much you owe. The number is probably higher than you think. Let it startle you. You need a wakeup call.

2. Tell somebody. Don't keep it a secret any longer. Shine light on the problem by telling someone you trust. Ask them to hold you accountable and discourage you from more spending binges.

3. Pinpoint the times when you are most vulnerable. Think back to the last time you spent emotionally. What emotion triggered the spending? How about the time before that? Get clear so you can do this next step…

4. Make a plan to respond rather than react. When an uncomfortable feeling shows up, pause for a moment and refuse to react by spending to temporarily numb that feeling. Instead, make an intentional choice to respond by doing something more productive.

Now is the time to decide what that healthier response might look like. Make a list of things that nourish your spirit, make you happy, and authentically boost your confidence. For example, perhaps instead of shopping, you decide to go to the park with your kids, visit a free museum exhibition, or invite a friend over to watch a movie or chat. *Experiences* with the people in your life make you much happier than buying more stuff. The happier you are, the less often you'll experience the kinds of feelings that drive you to spend emotionally.

Money Answers All Things

I remember the first time I read the scripture from the book of Ecclesiastes that suggests that money answers everything. At first, I was shocked. That is, until I gained a deeper understanding.

A feast is made for laughter, wine makes life merry, and money is the answer for everything (Ecclesiastes 10:19).

My pastor at the time said he was hesitant to quote the verse because people can greatly misinterpret it, but his bottom line was this: Money can solve any problem related to *things*. It will not solve most relationship issues (although having more of it could relieve some stress from your relationship). It will not solve most health issues (although it will buy you health insurance or better health care). But if you need food or shelter or clothing or someone to help you handle just about any project you want done—at home or in the marketplace—money will answer your problem.

I recall a partnership that nearly devastated my business in my twenties. The week it happened felt like the worst week of my life. I spent hours dealing with the issue and trying to come up with ways to rectify the problem. The following week my mother almost died. Suddenly, the issue in my business looked miniscule. As my mother lay in a coma, I told a friend, "If money can solve your problems, you don't really have any problems." You can negotiate or earn your way out of a money issue, but there's not much you can do when someone you love lies lifeless in a hospital bed.

How to Make Your Money Make You Happier

In my book *Successful Women Think Differently*, I shared three ways researchers have shown money can make you happier: If you can pay your bills, if you make more than the average income in your area, or if you give some away. Your money and how you choose to handle it can have a dramatic impact on your happiness.

I have long been passionate about women and money. Too many women, even well-educated ones, lack financial savvy. Some of this is due to the lack of financial education in our school systems and colleges. Very few schools teach students even the basics of money— how to balance a checking account, what an interest rate is, or how to save and plan for retirement. But even if schools taught the basics, it wouldn't be enough to make you happier. When it comes to money and happiness, there are some happiness habits every woman should aim for. Some of these may seem easy. Others may seem out of reach, depending on your financial situation. As you read them, open your mind to the fact that all of them are possible for you—even if they take a while to attain. Some of these habits may bring up emotions for you or challenge what you were taught about money as it relates to women. Don't let the emotions stop you.

8 Ways Money Can Trigger Your Happiness

1. *Live below your means.*

If you've ever been in a position of not being able to pay your bills or afford the basics, you know it is extremely stressful. Living below your means makes you happier. It also gives you a sense of control in your life that leaves you feeling confident about your ability to manage your finances. There is a deep satisfaction in that. You may have noticed the declaration at the beginning of this chapter: "I aim to live on less than

75 percent of my income." In focus groups with women, some were wide-eyed at this idea, as though it was impossible. You might not be in a position to do it today, but make it a goal to begin widening the gap between how much you make and how much you spend so that you consume less and less of your income each month. It feels good and creates a sense of relaxation and security when you have breathing room. This is what living below your means gives you. So if right now, you're living on 105 percent, make it your goal to get to 95 percent this year. If you are living on 95 percent, make a goal to get to 85 percent. As you earn more, the gap widens. And as you adjust your spending, the gap widens more. Instead of planning for the next car you're going to buy, you get excited about seeing how long you can make your current car last after you pay it off. My prayer for you is that you can live on half your income, and that one day you'll retire financially independent. With the right money choices, choices that make you happier or more secure, it's possible.

2. Be meek.

Feeling below average doesn't make a woman happy. While this may sound like pride, research shows that 76 percent of people, if given the option between two salaries and two towns, would rather make less money as long as they made twice as much as the average person in their town. This means being financially savvy isn't just about living below your means, but about putting yourself in environments that do not leave you feeling like you don't measure up. So don't buy the house in the most expensive neighborhood you can qualify for. Be meek. Spend *less* than you are capable of spending. It'll make you happier.

3. Give some away!

Giving, not receiving, is the way to happiness. As you know, service is a happiness trigger. So is giving financially. This is why the principle of tithing—giving ten percent or more of your income to God— is so significant. But beyond that, are you generous? Generous people are happier people. They do not allow fear to cause them to hold too tightly to their money and possessions. Instead, they approach life with an open hand that is willing to share with others. And because their hand is open to give, they often receive blessings far more valuable in return.

Whenever you get an unexpected windfall, always share some of it. Research shows that employees who share some of their bonus to help someone or donate to a charity report more happiness than those who do not. Who could you bless right now? Maybe the windfall wasn't just so you could buy those shoes you've been eyeing. Maybe it was also so you could bless your friend with something nice. You know that with her tight budget, she doesn't have a dime left over at the end of the month.

4. Buy experiences, not things.

When you have expendable income, take a look at the happiness triggers in this book and identify an experience you want to create. For example...

- Novelty. Is there something new you want to try?
- Savoring. Is there a meal you want to savor at your favorite restaurant with someone you can have stimulating conversation with?
- Play. Is it time to head to the beach or hit the slopes?
- Environment. Can you finally get that piece of art you'd love to hang in the living room and gaze at every time you walk by?

5. Negotiate.

As women, we are notorious for not negotiating—whether it is for the car we want or the job that was just offered. In fact, one of the rarely discussed reasons for the persistent gap between men's and women's pay could be the fact that men are much more likely than women to negotiate. In a study of almost 2,500 job seekers by the National Bureau of Economic Research, it was found that when an employer does not explicitly state that wages are negotiable, men are more likely than women to negotiate. But when an employer explicitly mentions the possibility that wages are negotiable, women are as likely and sometime slightly more likely to negotiate. So the pay gap between men and women is significantly more pronounced in jobs where wage negotiation is ambiguous.

What does this mean for you? It means you could be leaving money on the table for the same amount of work you are already doing.

6. Don't take anything for granted.

The more you have, the easier it is to become ungrateful. In the chapter on the happiness trigger of gratitude we'll explore the concept of hedonic adaptation, which is our tendency to adapt to increasingly better circumstances so that we need increasingly more to be happy. You can counter hedonic adaptation by being intentional about appreciating your blessings, savoring what you have, and refusing to take anything you have for granted. Gratitude holds the key to curbing your spending and leaves you feeling rich no matter how much money is in your bank account.

7. Buy time.

Would it make you happier to have more time? Whether it's time with friends and family or time for rest or to do the things you love most, having more time for what matters most will make you measurably happier. So when you have the expendable income, remember that spending it on things that will save you time or buy you time is a wise choice. A few examples of buying time include hiring a cleaning service, paying someone to cut the grass, or even paying a little more for where you live so that you cut 15 minutes off of your commute. Let's say you have a 45-minute commute from the time you leave your driveway until the time you walk through the door at work, but if you moved closer to work, you could cut the commute to 15 minutes. That's 30 minutes each way each day. That's five hours per week. The average American takes three weeks per year of vacation (but I recommend four!) so let's say you commute 48 weeks per year. That would give you an extra 240 hours per year to reclaim for yourself! What would you do with an extra 240 hours? In vacation time, that's 30 8-hour days of vacation.

If you decided to use the time to go to sleep 30 minutes earlier and wake up 30 minutes later, that would be the equivalent of 30 more full nights of sleep over the course of the year. And some of the extra cost of moving to a place that is slightly more expensive could be offset by the drop in how much you spend at the gas tank now that you live closer to work. Whenever you consider whether it is worth saving money by doing something that is a little less convenient, be sure not just to add the financial cost, but the time cost as well.

8. Pay now, enjoy later.

We are bombarded constantly with messages that tell us to "enjoy now, pay later." Elizabeth Dunn, a psychology professor at the University of British Columbia, and Michael Norton, a marketing professor at Harvard Business School, point this out in their book *Happy Money:* "Delaying consumption allows spenders to reap the pleasures of anticipation without the buzzkill of reality. Vacations provide the most happiness before they occur." The remedy? Pay for stuff, whether a spa treatment or your vacation, before you experience it. Spending money triggers areas of the brain that produce pain. This is why paying with cash results in spending less money than if you had paid with a credit card. So when you have something enjoyable planned, pay in advance. That way your brain will be free of the "payment pain" when it comes time to enjoy the experience. You will also be more likely to plan your spending and stick to a budget when you pay ahead of time.

Working Women

It was the fifth rainy day in a row. My head was spinning from a work schedule that requires me to change gears a lot. One day I'm writing, the next I'm on a plane for a speaking engagement, the next I'm doing a television interview, two client meetings, and a strategic marketing plan all on the same day. And that's just the work stuff.

On this particular day, two cute little boy toddlers waved at me from behind the fenced bars of the nursery playground in my building. Their little hands twirled back and forth as they looked at me, bright-eyed and innocent. "Bye-bye!" they said. "Buh-bye!" Never mind I was walking *into* the building and not out. "Hello" would have been the adult greeting, but bye-bye was much cuter. I smiled and waved back, "Bye-bye!" The toddlers behind them were sliding down slides, wandering aimlessly and contentedly around the colorful playground. Others were laughing into the air for no reason at all. And a part of me wanted to step onto the playground—not to get on the merry-go-round, but to step off it.

As much as I love what I do, there are moments of wanting to do absolutely nothing. Have you ever been there? Fortunately, I also have quite a few days where I stay home, do nothing, or take a vacation. After years of working for myself, I have been able to adjust my schedule to have breaks and flexibility.

In 2012, Forbes.com reported that 84 percent of working women told *ForbesWoman* and *The Bump* that "staying home to raise children is a financial luxury they aspire to." Many women—especially moms—are open to the idea of stepping right off the professional merry-go-round. This is especially evident among Generation X women. While many of their mothers took a few weeks' maternity leave and headed right back to work, many GenXers are more likely to stop working for at least a few years after having children. Perhaps it is because they watched their moms "having it all" and decided to opt for something different. Based on Forbes' survey, even the ones who do not step out of the workforce long to do so.

- Why do you think so many professional women today are stepping out of the workforce? What feelings do they wrestle with?

- What is the point of earning a law or graduate degree (or even a bachelor's degree) if you are not going to work?

- Do you ever feel so overwhelmed by the demands of work and personal life that the idea of a super-early retirement sounds enticing?

- What is so magical about working 40 hours a week? Could our society (and you!) be as productive if full-time meant a 25, 30, or 35-hour work week?

Why You Don't Want What You Wanted!

One of the most telling truths about happiness is that we are pretty poor predictors of what will actually make us happy. We truly believe that if we just had that job or that house or that relationship, we'd be happy. But often, once we get it, the reality of what is required to have that thing and keep it sets in. You may have done a happy dance at first, but now you're living it up close, every day. And when it comes to career, some women find that the amount and pressure of work—coupled with responsibilities at home—is more than what they wanted. You wanted to use your strengths and land the position, but you didn't want it to consume your life. You wanted the business, but you didn't think it had to mean giving up any semblance of a personal life. You wanted to be the boss, but you didn't have any idea that managing people can be like herding cats. So it may not be that you didn't want what you have, but maybe you just didn't want so much of it.

For example, I love strawberry cake. I mean, *love it.* But if forced to eat a whole strawberry cake every day, not only will I eventually hate the taste of it, but there are a few other unwanted results I'll experience—most of them horrible for my health. The same holds true when your schedule of previously desired activities begins to overwhelm you. What you once enjoyed begins to feel like a burden rather than something you get to do. The stress of it begins to take its toll.

Why 40 Hours?

What's so magical about the 40-hour work week? If work over-stresses you, I'd like to challenge you for a moment to imagine a more flexible, less strenuous work arrangement. Now, if you love your career, your business, or your job just as it is, this doesn't apply to you. But if you sometimes daydream about having more time for yourself, your family, and the dreams you have for your life, just humor me for a moment. Much of the way we live our lives is determined by what we have been taught is the norm. And most people never question that norm or attempt to forge a path that looks different from it.

But what if you decided to forge a path uniquely designed for the life you were created to live? What would that look like? Would you work 40 hours a week or 20 hours? Or would you choose not to work at all? Would you work from home or an office or behind the wheel of a delivery truck? And what adjustments, if any, would you need to make to your lifestyle in order to accommodate the work situation you desire?

As you ponder what will actually make you happy, don't be afraid to break outside the mold you may have fit yourself into your entire career. Most people follow what's normal and acceptable and believe they have no other choice. But with planning, creativity, and the faith to believe your life can be different, you can carve out a new way to work and live.

First, the planning. For most women, the financial considerations are the biggest obstacle to a less strenuous work schedule. Three considerations stand out most:

- How much you earn
- How much you need to cover expenses
- How much you have available in savings, investments, or residual income

We live in a culture that actively encourages debt. We are bombarded with messages that suggest we constantly need something bigger and better than what we have. If you buy into those messages, you can find yourself in bondage, unable to make new and better choices for how you want to spend your time because your obligations are so burdensome that the only choice you have is to stay right where you are. This is not everyone's story, but it is the story of too many women. If it is your story and you feel stuck, I encourage you to begin imagining the possibility that your life could be different. Here are a few ideas to get you started:

- Aim to create a work arrangement that fits you and your needs, even if it does not look like the arrangement of everyone around you. This may not happen overnight, but begin painting the vision and setting the wheels in motion to eventually achieve it.

- Rather than allowing yourself to burn out, work productively and in moderation. Work hard, but take breaks. Breathe. Stop overdoing it.

- Decide what you are willing to give up in order to have the type of schedule that will give you more breathing space. Think radically. Would you be willing to find a less expensive living arrangement? Get rid of the extra car? Forgo a promotion for now?

- Get quiet and listen for God's direction about your schedule. Then make adjustments accordingly.

Everything on Your Shoulders

A friend I'll call Peggy, a 48-year-old mom of three adult children, called as she headed home from work one Thursday evening. Peggy's been divorced for ten years and would like to be married again someday. A recruiter had contacted her earlier in the day about a potential job opportunity…2,000 miles away in Boise. Now, I've been to Boise. It's a lovely city—truly. Fresh air, open-minded people, beautiful scenery. But it is nowhere near Peggy's family or friends or anything she's trying to do at this time in her life. But she's tired of her current job, so she's considering her options. Talk of Boise sent her over the edge.

"I need a husband!" she demanded jokingly. "If I was married, moving to a far-off city wouldn't be so bad. We'd have each other. Or I'd just quit this job I'm sick and tired of and find something else to do right here in this city. But I can't! Everything is on my shoulders. *I just want somebody to take care of me! Is that so awful?*"

These aren't the words we expect to hear from a financially secure woman, are they? But over and over, I've heard them. Remember that

84 percent of working women say that being able to stay home is a financial luxury they aspire to? What's more, one in three resent their partner for not earning enough to make that dream a reality.

As opportunities have opened up for women in the last 40 years, we've proven that we can excel. We can certainly make it on our own—but the question is, do we want to?

This may not sound politically correct, but even among the most financially secure, women like to feel taken care of. If this isn't you, fine. But for most of us, feeling "covered" by a man is natural. That covering includes physical protection, financial security, and emotional support. Consider the biblical description of the responsibilities of a husband. He is clearly told to care for the woman as much as he cares for himself. She is to feel wholly protected and covered by his love for her—even to the point of him giving his life for her:

> Husbands, love your wives, just as Christ loved the church and gave himself up for her...Husbands ought to love their wives as their own bodies. He who loves his wife loves himself. After all, no one ever hated their own body, but they feed and care for their body, just as Christ does the church (Ephesians 5:25,28-29).

That is a tremendous love. It is a love meant to be equal to Christ's love. If that is the kind of love a wife is created for, is it any wonder that a woman craves so deeply to be cared for even when she is doing an amazing job of caring for herself?

In her groundbreaking book *For Women Only*, author Shaunti Feldhahn discusses the deeply entrenched feelings men have about providing for their wives. Speaking to women about her findings, she said, "Even if you made enough income to support your family's lifestyle, it would make no difference to the mental burden your husband feels to provide." In numerous interviews with men, she admits she was startled by men's feelings on the topic. "Whatever a man's wife felt about it, whatever she did or didn't earn, he felt that providing was *his job*. Period." In fact, in a scientific survey, she and other researchers discovered that 78 percent of men said they would still feel a compulsion to provide even if their wife's income alone was able to provide for the family. This percentage was consistent among men whether married or single, religious or nonreligious, old or young. And the compulsion was even stronger among men from minority groups.[1]

If this is how men are wired, perhaps it is no surprise that so many women feel a desire to be provided for—even if they can provide for themselves. And is it possible, then, that when we feel the pressure to provide entirely for ourselves (out of necessity) that that pressure creates a level of stress that feels different for us than it does for men? Most men feel a duty to provide. Big brothers are told to watch out for little sisters. Good fathers are compelled to cover their daughters—especially the unmarried ones. Healthy sons feel compelled to cover their divorced, unmarried, or widowed moms. It is a natural instinct.

This is not to say every man does this. But it is to say that the majority of men feel a compulsion to protect the women closest to them.

As a financially savvy woman, recognize that even if you are financially secure, you are not alone if sometimes you wish you had someone else to help you carry the load. If you don't have that support, refuse to allow it to become justification for a pity party. In the last half century, financial doors have opened to women as a result of opportunities in education and the workplace. Be intentional about your money. The gratification of being a good steward, the joy of using your money for good, and the peace that comes from building a stable financial life are all seeds that will blossom into a happier life.

Activate This Happiness Trigger!

- Spend less than you are capable of spending, not the maximum. Give yourself some financial margin.

- Next time you buy a gift or reward yourself, choose to buy an experience rather than a product or material thing.

- Negotiate. It feels good to stand up for yourself and get more than what is offered, whether buying something you want or landing a new position.

- Make it your goal to increase the margin between what you make and what you spend so that you live on 75 percent or less of your income.
- Find somebody to bless who needs it. Be generous.

When a Woman Makes More Money than Her Honey

How do money and career impact relationship happiness?

Points to Ponder:

- Today, women earn more money than their husbands in nearly 40 percent of American households.

- Studies show that when women are financially dependent on their husbands, they are more loyal. However, when men are financially dependent on their wives, they are more likely to cheat.

- A 30-year-old woman today is more than three times as likely to be unmarried as she was in the 1970s.

Conversation Starters:

- Some couples thrive with the wife earning more income. What do you think is the difference between those couples who are happy and those who struggle?

- Some women say men are "intimidated" by them. Is this because the men are truly intimidated or is it something else?

- What would you do if the issue of "who makes more" began to affect the happiness of your relationship?

How do you feel about making more money than your spouse or significant other? Do you believe men are intimidated by a woman making more money or is that just an excuse women use to explain away deeper issues that are driving men away? These are questions very few women had to answer in 1970 because very few women out-earned men in that era. But today, the tide has turned and it creates very real feelings and frustrations that can affect your happiness—whether you are married or you want to be. If you are a working woman, there is a chance that you make more than your mate (or future mate).

Katie's husband had not had a full-time job for nearly three years, and she was wary of his "efforts" to land a full-time job. He was laid off from his position as an engineer, and after more than a year of search-ing for a job, he stopped seriously looking. Then he got comfortable. Although they had not agreed to Katie carrying all the financial weight of the family, it seemed her husband was content to let her do so. "Why not?" seemed to be his attitude. She earned a good salary and with the low cost of living in Indiana, her salary covered the bills. Katie had become disgusted with her husband's loss of motivation to work, and had just about given up on any hope of the situation changing. "At this point, I'd settle for him getting a full-time job at minimum wage. I just want him to *work*."

I felt sad for Katie. She's a hard worker. She loves her family. She seemingly did all the right things. Married nearly 20 years with two teenagers, she was a sales executive in a male-dominated field and had persevered through unfair treatment. In the early days of her career, she'd been passed over for promotions in favor of less-experienced men, but through tenacity and faith finally arrived at a point in her career where she felt well-compensated and appreciated for her efforts. Most of her married life, she and her husband earned about the same salary and shared the financial responsibilities. She respected her husband and often bragged about how great he was at figuring things out and how methodical he was at finding creative solutions to problems— traits she attributed to him being an engineer.

An October 2012 cover story in the *Atlantic* called "Rich Wives, Poor Husbands," asked some intriguing questions. The article pointed out that in the United States today, almost 40 percent of wives earn more money than their husbands. The result seems to be a host of complicated, if not surprising issues. Perhaps you've experienced some of these issues yourself or observed them in your circle of friends and coworkers. One recent study showed that when a woman's financial contribution to the household exceeds 60 percent, the marriage is more likely to end in divorce.[2]

Some of these statistics surely correlate with all of the opportunities that came to women beginning in the 1970s. Today, for every two men who graduate from college, three women do. Women are more likely to earn graduate degrees and most managers today—believe it or not—are women. Looking to the future, the financial dynamics of marriages are likely to lean more and more toward women out-earning men. For the first time in history, a growing number of women under 30 are earning more than their male counterparts. And the decline in manufacturing, a field that empowered millions of men to earn middle-class incomes and support their families as the sole breadwinner through the 1970s, has taken a tremendous toll on the employment of men without college degrees. Many of the career fields with the highest growth potential today are female-dominated career paths such as nursing and health care.

Why Does It Matter?

In theory, it shouldn't matter, right? And for many women, it doesn't. Perhaps you are a woman who earns more than her husband, and it has never created any challenges in the dynamics of your relationship. *I hope that's the case.* But research and my experience coaching hundreds of women has shown that in many relationships—or even in many women's desire for a relationship—financial success (or even perceived financial success) can sometimes create frustrating roadblocks.

Men define themselves much more by their careers than women do. Just as women are wired for relationship, men are wired to provide. In fact, long-term unemployment (one year or more) has a more devastating impact on a man than it does a woman. Studies show it takes as much as five years for him to fully recover—longer than it takes to recover from the death of a spouse. That is remarkable. If so much of his identity is tied to his ability to provide, what does it do to the average man when he cannot provide?

In Katie's case, heated discussions about her husband's job search—or lack thereof—revealed a seething resentment and insecurity underlying his behavior. After a year of trying hard but failing to land a position, he felt dejected. He began to internalize the failure and eventually gave up hope, although he did not express his hopelessness to his wife. In the several years preceding his layoff, she had already begun to inch ahead of him professionally. Opportunities finally began to open for Katie that had previously been shut. Meanwhile, her husband felt stuck and unable to break through to the next level. After a while, he quit expecting to move up the ladder anytime soon and settled into his fate as a middle manager. His complacency, according to Katie, may have contributed to his layoff. When the company made decisions about who to keep and who to let go, they considered performance evaluations over the previous two years and his were average. He felt defeated. His efforts to excel at work had failed. He didn't manage to keep his job. He couldn't manage to get another job. Meanwhile, his wife was promoted and sailing along just fine in her career. He'd become competitive with her—and felt he'd lost. In counseling, he admitted that he felt his decision to let his wife carry the financial burden alone was a sort of punishment for her success. *Ouch.*

Katie and her husband's situation reflects the kind of real-life dynamics that can sabotage marital happiness. Of course, this isn't the case in every situation, but it does happen. In Katie's case, she made a decision to persevere in her marriage. She doesn't describe it as entirely happy, but she is quick to point out her husband's positive qualities. He's a nurturing father to their 17-year-old son and 15-year-old daughter (although she is concerned about what the relationship dynamic is teaching them). He is a dynamite cook. And he has agreed to individual therapy and marriage counseling to deal with the challenges they face in the marriage.

In my interviews with women around the country, I encountered a number whose salaries exceed their husbands. For some, it is a nonissue. For example, Jennifer enjoys going to her job each day while her husband stays home with the children. "It works for us," she says. "But I realize I've got a unique husband. He is very secure and comfortable with who he is. We decided one of us should stay home while the kids are too young for school. And I was in a more stable position professionally and I enjoy my job, so we decided I would keep working."

But Angela, who is now retired, had a different experience. "I was making about $54,000 per year in my job as a marketing manager. My husband was a supervisor in a plant, a job that paid about $10,000 less than mine. He would work crazy hours just to get overtime so that I would not make more money. As long as his salary was $1,000 more than mine for the year, he was okay. He couldn't take the idea that I made more." Angela's story might be extreme, but it points to another dynamic that can occur: competition. Angela was not competing with her husband. However, her husband felt compelled to compete with her.

Rachel said she did not earn more than her husband, but she still found herself in an awkward discussion with him about the perception that she earned more. "I think people think we have our lifestyle because of your income," he complained one day. "When we go to parties, they're always asking about your business, but they rarely take an interest in my work." Rachel expressed frustration at the criticism and mixed messages she received. At one point, she offered to give up her business and stay home. But her husband insisted she keep doing the work she loved. "I think he wanted to be supportive, but no matter how much I praised him and bragged about him to friends and family, he seemed to feel that my accomplishments somehow diminished his," she recalls. She is no longer married.

Can He Meet Your Expectations?

Sometimes it is not a matter of whether a man can provide, but whether he can provide at the level he imagines a woman expects. So if you are dating, the question becomes, "What are his perceptions of your expectations?" If he perceives he cannot please you at the level of his ability to provide, he may choose not to pursue you. I emphasize the word "perceives" because often what a man perceives as your expectation may not actually be your expectation. However, perception becomes reality. If you are open to a mate who makes less, does he perceive you are really okay with that? Or does he perceive that he won't be able to meet your expectations? If you are not okay with it, are you clear about why?

A woman's feelings on this issue can be very personal. You may even find yourself feeling apologetic about your feelings. You may have been raised believing that a man is supposed to provide. You may have worked hard to excel professionally and financially and always assumed your mate would still be your financial knight in shining armor. "My mother always worked," a 22-year-old recent college graduate explained to me. "But 'her' money was for whatever she wanted to use it for—as well as family vacations, savings, or extras that we wanted. I was raised that the husband was responsible for covering the household financially."

Now, that might sound like a fairy tale to many women today, but just a few decades ago, that sort of arrangement was more of the norm. If you grew up as a girl in a household with that financial arrangement, your feelings about men and money are bound to be affected. Whatever your experience growing up, your unique set of experiences is bound to shape your attitudes and expectations.

The good news is that as an adult, you can intentionally shape your attitude and expectations. If an attitude adjustment is needed, only you can make that decision. As you seek to be happy while you navigate financial dynamics, do the following:

- Explore your feelings. What points struck a nerve with you in this section? Write down your beliefs on money and relationships and then ask, "Are these beliefs helping me or hurting me? Is there an attitude I'd like to change?"

- If the financial dynamics are creating problems in your relationship, don't pretend nothing is wrong. Have a conversation with your mate to work through it.

- If you are not in a relationship but want to be, look for a man who will celebrate your professional and financial accomplishments and feel confident in his own.

Gratitude

*How the art of appreciation causes you to work
out more, sleep better, and be less agitated*

Decision:

"Before I lay my head down at night, I reflect on the three
best things about today."

I had a friend once who complained that I said *thank you* too much. "In my family, we don't say thank you for things you're supposed to do," he explained.

I found that odd. "In my family," I responded, "we say thank you for the stuff you're supposed to do because in some families, people don't do what they're supposed to. We're just grateful for family who does—so we say, 'Hey, thank you for taking me to the airport today… taking out the trash this morning…reminding me that it's Aunt Billie's birthday so I didn't forget to call her!'" That relationship didn't go far, but my penchant for gratitude has produced a great deal of happiness in my life. I didn't realize it at the time because I had no knowledge of what my happiness triggers are, but gratitude is in my top three.

I am naturally grateful. I sit on my deck and feel thankful that the birds saw fit to chirp this morning; their sound is music to my ears. I stand in the shower and as the warm water jets effortlessly out of the showerhead, I feel grateful that I came along in the late twentieth century—not burdened with drawing water to take cold baths in an iron tub after two or three other family members have already bathed. Ugh.

I don't know if other people think about such things, but I do. I am keenly aware, for example, that just waking up in America gives me a myriad of blessings for which to be grateful, even on days when life may feel like it's upside-down. Gratitude mostly comes easily for me. I say "mostly" because I am indeed human. And I have my moments when I too need to be reminded just how good life is.

The expression of gratitude is not simply for the benefit of the recipient—although being appreciated feels good. The expression of gratitude largely benefits the giver. It is an act that creates positive emotion in us that measurably boosts happiness. While Scripture promises time and again that God loves praise and commands thankfulness, the truth of the matter is that when you take the time to stop and thank him for the things for which you are grateful, it elevates *you*.

When my mother returned home after a two-month stay in the hospital following a massive brain aneurysm and brain surgery, I believe it was her attitude and expressions of gratitude that empowered and energized her to recover. As she engaged in physical therapy, speech therapy, and occupational therapy and attempted to regain her sight, speech, balance, and ability to walk and swallow, she said repeatedly, "At least I have the chance to get better. I'm grateful for that." With that gratitude she focused on her recovery, determined to make the most of the opportunity before her to get better. And she did.

"We are most alive in those moments when our hearts are conscious of our treasures." – *Thornton Wilder*

What Is Gratitude?

Gratitude is simply the expression of thankfulness for the blessings of life. Gratitude is about others. It is an act of humility that acknowledges we could not be who we are or where we are without the generosity and contribution of others. It is also the recognition that there is good in the world, that God's grace and love abounds. Throughout the Bible, God calls us to gratitude. "I will give thanks to you, Lord, with all my heart; I will tell of all your wonderful deeds" Psalm 9:1 says.

Why Gratitude Counteracts Negativity

Incomes in the U.S., Great Britain, and Japan have doubled over the last 50 years. Yet happiness has not measurably increased. One of the reasons may be something called hedonic adaptation. As you get used to having more, you no longer see your gains as a big deal. That is, unless you are intentionally grateful. When most middle-class families shared one car, it was obvious why you should be grateful if your family had two. In fact, most homes that had a garage or carport in the 1960s had one that fit a single car. But if you have a two- or three-car garage, the expectation is that you ought to have two or three cars to fill it! That's the norm. So it may not occur to you to notice that there are people right in your own city who do not have a car—some who may want one, but for any number of reasons cannot afford one right now.

Turn on the television. Glance up at the billboards. Open your favorite magazine. Launch your Internet browser. You are bombarded with images of what you ought to have and the suggestion that everyone else already has it. The materialism of our age is poisonous to an attitude of gratitude. Your antidote is to intentionally notice the good in your life.

The Antidote to the Hedonic Treadmill

In *Successful Women Think Differently*, I talked about an effect called the "hedonic treadmill." It is rooted in the fact that we are generally poor predictors of what will make us happy. We repeatedly seek out things we believe will make us happy. When we get them, although there may be a temporary boost in happy feelings, we eventually become used to them. Having the thing we thought would make us happy becomes our new normal. We adjust to the improving circumstances. So we seek out the next thing we believe we need in order to be happy. From a new house to a new spouse, if you don't learn to be grateful for what you have when you have it, you may learn the hard way that the grass is not usually greener on the other side.

"Counting one's blessings may directly counteract the effects of hedonic adaptation, the process by which our happiness level returns, again and again, to its set-point, by preventing people from taking the good things in their lives for granted," says gratitude researcher and University of California at Davis professor Dr. Robert Emmons in his book *Thanks! How the New Science of Gratitude Can Make You Happier*. "If we consciously remind ourselves of our blessings, it should become harder to take them for granted and adapt to them."

I've learned that gratitude can keep me from buying things I don't need. Case in point: My car is 11 years old. I could buy a new one, but why? I like the one I have. It runs just fine. The only money I spend on it goes to tune-ups and oil changes—and, of course, car insurance. It gets me where I need to go. Just the other day I managed to fit an entire futon in it and drive it to my younger brother's new apartment with a half-inch to spare when I closed the trunk. Granted, my mother was a little squished sitting in the passenger seat since I'd moved the seat as far up as it could go, but we got a laugh out of that. When I bought the car I never assumed I'd keep it as long as I have, but I'm content. One day, when I need it or really want it, I'll buy something else. But for now, I am satisfied. I have gratitude to thank for that, and an authentic confidence that knows I am not defined by the year, make, and model of what I drive.

Wanting what you have is a hallmark of happiness, and in particular, gratitude. "Grateful people are mindful materialists," Dr. Emmons explains. "Deliberate appreciation can reduce the tendency to depreciate what one has, making it less likely that the person will go out and replace what they have with newer, shinier, faster, better alternatives." Do you want what you have? If not, can you find some reasons to appreciate your belongings and be content until circumstances allow you to have something different?

There is a certain ease of life that occurs when you don't always feel like you are on pins and needles waiting for life to come together. There is a joy that comes when you embrace your current circumstances. And I believe God is present in that joy. There are so many scriptures about being thankful, it simply cannot be ignored. I especially love 1 Thessalonians 5:16-18. "Rejoice always, pray continually, give thanks in all circumstances; for this is God's will for you in Christ Jesus."

It is God's will that we be thankful. This isn't just about you being happier. It is about God's will for you—to appreciate what you have rather than focusing on what you don't. Noticing what you have to be thankful for will always point you in the right spiritual direction—and it will always lift your spirits.

Gratitude Is Good Medicine

Feeling down? Having trouble sleeping? Catch colds easily? You might be surprised at the simple habit researchers now say keeps you happier, healthier, and better rested: counting your blessings. In studies by researchers at the University of California at Davis, participants who wrote down three blessings every day were compared to those who did not. The more grateful group had stronger immune systems, caught fewer colds, had less trouble falling asleep and staying asleep, and felt better about their lives. They were even more likely to exercise. Interestingly, it's not enough to simply say what you are grateful for. You must write it down, according to researchers. Apparently, there is power in the written word.

To start your gratitude habit, keep a notebook at your bedside. When you get up, ask yourself a simple question that evokes gratitude, such as, "What three things do I most look forward to today?" or "What three things am I most grateful for today?" Or write in your gratitude journal before going to sleep—a practice that has been shown to improve sleep habits. Rather than counting sheep to cure insomnia, try counting your blessings. Ask, "What are the three best things that happened to me today?" or "What did I most appreciate today?"

There are other benefits to keeping a gratitude journal, according to the research, including feeling more alert and energized and being more willing to give emotional support to others. So grab a notebook or journal this week and start making note of what you are grateful for.

Do You Know How to Give Thanks?

Besides expressing thankfulness to God, it is essential to learn how to thank the people in your life. Not flippantly and without emotion, but genuinely and warmly. Even a simple thank-you can be powerful when you look the recipient in the eye, squeeze their hand, and say, "Thank you. I appreciate what you did for me. It meant so much to me when…" Too often in today's world, we miss the opportunity to express gratitude meaningfully so the person you are talking to *feels* your gratitude.

I've noticed it can take a bit of vulnerability to express gratitude authentically. When you express gratitude to someone, you are in essence acknowledging that they did something good for you. The more meaningful the gift—whether the gift of time or thoughtfulness or material goods—the more powerful its impact on you, and the more powerful an authentic thank-you will be.

Why is it that we sometimes hold back on expressing just exactly how someone else's generosity affected us? It is easy to simply say *thank you*. And often, that is all that is necessary. But there are degrees of expression, sincerity, and emotion that can go into a thank-you. Be intentional. Sometimes, going beyond thank-you to state *why* the giver's gesture was meaningful to you and how it impacted you can bless the person on the receiving end.

"Thank you for listening to me vent last night. I needed someone to talk to and appreciate the way you listen without trying to solve the problem or tell me not to feel what I'm feeling."

"Thank you for keeping my kids last week. I know you had a very hectic week, and I really appreciate your taking the time."

"Thank you for all the work you put into that project. You went well above my expectations and I appreciate the way you did the work with excellence."

When you say thank you to someone for providing something meaningful to you, tell them not just "thank you," but why you are thankful.

Write a Gratitude Letter

One way to make a special, heartfelt impact on someone and also articulate for yourself someone's positive influence in your life is through a gratitude letter. It's simple. Think of someone who has blessed you to whom you would like to express a special thank-you and write a letter. In that letter, answer these questions:

- What did that person do for you?
- Why did it matter to you?
- What did they sacrifice or what effort did they put forth in providing the blessing to you?
- Why is it important to you now to express your gratitude?
- What do you want them to know that perhaps you have not said verbally before?

The power of a gratitude letter is not simply in the written words, but in the experience you can create by reading the letter aloud to the recipient. Make an event of it. It's a wonderful Thanksgiving ritual, birthday ritual, or milestone to mark a celebratory occasion. But of course, don't put it off until you find a good holiday. If you feel led to write one, do it today. Then pay a "gratitude visit" to the recipient and read it aloud to them.

Receiving Gratitude

At the end of the Coaching and Positive Psychology Institute's very first Coach Training Intensive in 2010, I was overwhelmed by a gift from the 42 students in attendance: a gratitude box. Each student handwrote a note of thanks expressing what the weekend-long training had meant to them. They gathered the thank-you notes in a box, tied a bow on it, and presented it to me. I waited until the next day to open it. I was exhausted from leading 16 hours of training in two days and wanted to fully experience and savor each note—and that would take energy. So I placed the box on my desk in my home office. The next morning I went downstairs, sat at my desk, and opened each note slowly and read it deliberately. The notes were heartfelt. Here are excerpts from a few:

- "This experience was amazing and this class mirrors your optimism and spunk!"
- "What can I say? Your mission statement isn't merely words on a page—you're living it…walking it out! Thank

you for the sacrifice of your time, your prayers, and your knowledge."

- "Today, my business is flying high due to the ways in which your courage to pursue your dreams has inspired me to pursue mine. Thank you so much for your love and your beauty—inside and out."

- "I commend you for acting on your vision continually."

- "Thank you, thank you for being obedient to God's call on your life."

- "Thanks for the aha's, shifts, breakthroughs, and revelations. I love you truly!"

- "My life has been forever changed! I'm on the right track."

- "You are such a blessing. This training was a dream come true!"

- "I hope our paths cross many more times!"

- "You were the example God gave me to become a life coach."

The notes were sincere. The gift was the epitome of the lessons I'd been teaching that weekend—lessons in gratitude, engagements, connection, and community. Not only had they gotten it, they were living it in their expressions of appreciation.

Soon, my tears flowed. I was overwhelmed that something I'd created had generated so much gratitude. It was confirmation that indeed the effort had been worth it. Lives had been changed. I was appreciated.

That box still sits in my office. And when I have a day when I feel frustrated or wonder if my efforts are worth it, I can go to my gratitude box and remember that the emphatic answer is *Yes!*

When someone thanks you, receive it. Never say, "Oh, no, don't thank me for that! It was nothing." A simple "You're welcome" acknowledges that even if it was nothing for you to do, it was a blessing to the recipient.

On a trip to speak in Tampa, Florida, I took a walk out to the water.

A long wooden walkway led from the hotel through trees and into the bay. At the end of the walkway was a gazebo I had seen from my hotel room. It was midday and no one else was around, so I lay down on a bench in the gazebo and pondered gratitude. I lay there and pondered each of the key areas of my life—relationships, finances, work, health, and spiritual life. *What do I have to be grateful for in each area?* I asked myself. One by one, I pondered. And I stumbled upon an amazing discovery. My life is better in each of those areas than it has ever been. (Well, almost. I'm not normally one to think much about my weight, but I weigh more than I ever have before—I've gained five pounds and want to get a six-pack.) But seriously, other than that, my life is the best it's ever been.

That is not to say it is perfect or that I do not have aspirations and goals for other things I would like to see unfold, but life is better than ever. I've learned and grown and made so much progress. I am happier in my relationships. I feel appreciated and understood, loved and cherished. I am better off financially and have no compulsion to spend emotionally. (This is big for me. Some people eat emotionally. I had to overcome spending emotionally.) I hear from God and feel totally inside his will for my life. I love what I do and am excited about the doors that are opening.

I lay in that gazebo astonished. How is it that my life could be better than ever—and until that moment, I had not consciously noticed it?

While it is essential to use gratitude to pull you up when your life isn't going as planned, it is just as important to use gratitude to notice just how blessed you are when life is going exactly the way you want it to. Is there an area of your life in which you are doing better than ever? Or shoot, maybe it's not better than ever, but it's better than it was! Acknowledge that. Thank God for it. Gratitude will wake you up to your amazing life.

Activate This Happiness Trigger!

- Write down three blessings before going to bed at night— as well as your reflection about what those blessings mean to you.

- Write a gratitude letter to someone who is a blessing to you, recounting in vivid detail what they did for you and why it was so meaningful to you. Choose a time to pay them a gratitude visit and read it aloud to them in person.

- In the mornings, ask yourself, "What am I grateful for today?"

- Write a thank-you note to someone for a good deed or gift or for simply being who they are.

- At work, take a moment to thank a coworker or client and acknowledge what it takes for them to do the work they do. For example, "You come in here every day with a smile on your face, no matter what. That always lifts me up and inspires me to have a better attitude. Thank you."

Facebook or Fakebook? The Problem with Upward Social Comparison

*Social media empowers everybody to
star in their own reality show*

Points to Ponder

- A reality television and social media culture has exponentially multiplied the number of people you compare yourself to. Upward social comparison drains your happiness.

- Reality shows are not reality, but that doesn't mean you won't be seduced by the illusion.

- Everyone shows you what they want you to see on social media and hides what they don't want you to see.

- Gratitude can keep you grounded when you feel tempted to make upward social comparisons.

Conversation Starters

- Have you ever felt worse after logging in to your social media account? How so? Why?

- What percentage of your social media friends have you spoken to over the last six months?

- What has the reality television culture taught women about how women should behave with one another and show themselves to the world?

Alexis logged in to Facebook one evening after getting home from work and scrolled through the news feed. Her fellow high school track buddy Ericka had posted an adorable video of her two-year-old daughter playing in the backyard. A colleague from her first job out of college posted a picture of her and her husband hiking with the caption, "My hubby is amazing. How lucky am I to have been his wife for 15 years. Love you, sweetie!" They were celebrating their fifteenth wedding anniversary at a cabin in the mountains. Her former roommate's sister Mia had just landed a promotion and posted her excitement "Promotion today! And a raise! I feel so blessed!" her post read. Alexis's coworker Barbara from accounting, a sweet woman in her sixties, had a new profile picture with her son at his graduation from medical school. He looked so happy in his cap and gown. It was all good news. Everybody's life looked spectacular and exciting. But that night, Alexis didn't cheer. She sat in front of her computer and cried.

"What's wrong with my life?" she thought. As she sat in front of the computer, wanting to post something interesting, she wondered what would happen if she posted the truth: "I suspect my husband is cheating on me with a coworker, my son just told me college isn't for him and he's dropping out, and my boss gave me an unfair review that's going to sabotage any hope that I'll get promoted in the next year!" How many people would click "like" on that post?

That night, Alexis shut down her account. She realized the constant peering into the online lives of people she never talked to, some whom she hadn't seen since graduating high school or college, was not a diversion from her problems. Instead, it made her feel worse about her problems by suggesting that no one else had any.

One of the most significant cultural shifts of the last decade is the extent and pace with which we can communicate and connect with an ever-increasing network of people, many of whom we never come into contact with in real life. From the 1950s through the 1990s, television gave us a 3D visual point of comparison of what life should look like based on the sitcoms and dramas that were presented. But today, real life and reality collide every day, not just on television, but on your computer, your tablet, your phone. You keep tabs on what everyone is doing—or supposedly doing—24/7. Research has shown repeatedly that happiness decreases when you're constantly comparing yourself to those you think are doing better than you. If your comparisons are balanced with comparisons to those who are not doing as well as you, the perspective keeps your happiness in check. But you are often more likely to notice those you envy than those who haven't yet attained what you already have.

The solution? Limit your exposure to constant upward social comparisons. And secondly, practice gratitude as a means of remaining aware of the blessings in your own life rather than obsessing over everyone else's.

Social media can be a powerful tool for reconnecting with old friends and staying in touch with current ones. However, if upward social comparisons begin to skew your perspective you know it's time to step back. That doesn't necessarily mean you need to opt out entirely, but perhaps for a while. The same can be said for your exposure to television shows that promote attitudes and values that leave you feeling stressed, anxious, and less appreciative of your own life and blessings.

Have you ever found yourself making upward comparisons to other people after watching a show or spending too much time online? After making comparisons, have you beat yourself up for not doing enough, being enough, or making enough progress in your own life? Be intentional about noticing how your exposure to media—whether online or traditional—shapes how you feel about life. And when you feel yourself getting out of balance, step back, take a breath, and get grounded in the reality of real life by noticing all you have to be grateful for.

Connection

*Why you are less connected, more anxious, and have
fewer close friends than women in previous generations*

Decision

"I speak to my family and friends more than I email and text them."

Janie's husband, Mike, came home from work early one evening excited. He had received a promotion at work he'd wanted for more than a year. He beamed as he walked in from the garage to the kitchen and announced the good news.

"You are not going to believe this!" he exclaimed with a smile on his face.

"What?" Janie said with a smile, her eyes stretched with anticipation and curiosity.

"I got the promotion! They finally gave me the promotion!"

"Oh my goodness!" she responded. "That's incredible!" Janie flung her arms around her husband's neck and gave him a big congratulatory kiss. "I am so proud of you."

"Wait, wait," he whispered with excitement. "That's not all."

Janie listened intently, smiling warmly and hoping that what she was anticipating was also what he was about to tell her. "There's more? What?" she probed.

"They also gave me a twelve thousand dollar raise!!!" he announced.

With that, Janie feigned passing out. Mike laughed. "I thought you were only expecting a five or six thousand dollar bump!" she said.

"You are quite the negotiator, honey. How'd you end up getting twice that amount?"

"Well, I gently mentioned I was underpaid in my last position and gave some other justifications based on my experience. They agreed!"

"Wow," Janie reflected. "You are amazing. So how do you feel?"

"Incredible," Mike admitted. "Like my hard work has been worth it, even though the promotion took longer than I wanted it to. I learned a lesson about perseverance. And God made up for the last year when I've felt a bit underpaid with this bigger-than-expected raise."

"Well," she said, "this deserves a special celebration! What do you want to do to mark this milestone? Maybe we can have a promotion party or something!"

"Hmm. I hadn't thought of that," he said as he pondered the idea of having a few friends and family over. "Let's have a cookout!"

"Done," Janie said. "Make a list of everybody you want to invite and I'll take care of the rest."

Mike's smile grew wider as he thought about having his favorite friends and his parents over. His dad would be so proud. "You know what?" he said to Janie. "I need to call my dad and a few others anyway to tell them the good news. So I'll invite them when I call." With that, he bounded out of the kitchen on cloud nine, more excited about the promotion than he first entered the kitchen.

Janie and Mike's conversation was like a synchronized dance that created an upward spiral of positive emotion. Mike entered the conversation with good news and Janie responded openly and enthusiastically, matching his excitement and giving him the safe space to get even more excited. Her approach is what researcher Shelly Gable calls "active constructive responding," a way of communicating with someone about good news that helps build connection. Relationship experts often talk about the importance of active listening as a relationship skill. But active constructive responding can be even more powerful. It combines active listening, effective praise, genuine enthusiasm, and powerful questions that help the person savor the good news. It strengthens the relationship by building the bonds of connection.

According to Dr. Gable, there are four ways of responding to good news, but active-constructive responses are the only responses that build connection. In fact, if you respond any of the other three ways, you actually erode connection. The four ways of responding are described here:

	Active	Passive
Constructive	"This is great. I know how important that promotion was to you! We should go out and celebrate and you can tell me what excited you most about your new job." Nonverbal communication: Maintaining eye contact and displays of positive emotion such as genuine smiling, touching, and laughing.	"That is good news." Nonverbal communication: Little to no active emotional expression.
Destructive	"That sounds like a lot of responsibility to take on. There will probably be more stress involved in the new position and longer hours at the office." Nonverbal communication: Displays of negative emotion such as furrowed brow and frowning.	"What are we doing on Friday night?" Nonverbal communication: Little to no eye contact, turning away, leaving room.

"Could a greater miracle take place than
for us to look through each other's eyes for
an instant?" – *Henry David Thoreau*

What Is Connection?

Connection can be summed up simply: It is love. It is those moments in which you connect heart to heart with another, whether the cashier at the grocery store or the coworker in the next cubicle or your husband in the midst of a petty argument. Love creates connection. When you truly connect, God is in the midst of it. How do I know this? God is love. So if connection is love, then to be connected is to experience God in our relationships. The more disconnected we are in our relationships, the less we experience God. Every moment with others is an opportunity for a momentary exchange of love. I am not talking about love in the romantic sense or even in the way that you might love a parent or a child or your best friend. I am talking about love in the sense that is described in 1 Corinthians 13. That kind of love is the expression of the following:

- Patience
- Kindness
- Humility
- Service
- Truthfulness
- Forgiveness
- Protection
- Trust
- Hope
- Perseverance

When each of these traits is expressed and also received, connection occurs. But connection is dependent on your expression of love also being received by the other person. If the other person chooses not to receive it, love has occurred, but not connection. The other person must be open to receiving your expression of love through one of the ten love traits described in 1 Corinthians 13:4-7:

> Love is patient, love is kind. It does not envy , it does not boast, it is not proud. It does not dishonor others, it is not self-seeking, it is not easily angered, it keeps no record of

wrongs. Love does not delight in evil but rejoices in the truth. It always protects, always trusts, always hopes, always perseveres.

Authentic connection energizes you. It elevates your soul and generates a synchronicity between you and the other person or people involved in the interaction.

Positive psychologist Chris Peterson summarized the power of relationships to impact happiness in a very simple way. "Other people matter," he often said. Indeed, it is true. Yes, you might be happy to get some solitude when you've been around too many people for too long. But sooner or later, you are going to need people. We are built for connection. In today's world, however, the ability to truly connect has become increasingly difficult.

Why Authentic Connection Is Getting Harder

There are several reasons why connection is getting harder in our culture today. It is important to recognize these reasons so you can counteract them in your own life. If you don't, your happiness is bound to be impacted. Here are seven factors that make it increasingly difficult:

1. Women are more mobile.

Forty or fifty years ago you were far more likely to live in or near the same city in which you grew up. Today, it is more likely that you live elsewhere. We are a more mobile society, which also means we have to connect with new people in new places—something that becomes more difficult as you leave your twenties when most of your peers are single and carefree.

2. More of us live alone than ever before.

If you live alone, you are not alone. About 32 million Americans live alone—and 17 million of them are women. In 1950, only four million Americans lived alone. In cities such as Denver, Seattle, and Cleveland, 40 percent of households have just one person living in them.

In New York City, nearly half of households fit that mold. Many of those who live alone prefer it that way, but it is isolating. In an article on cbsnews.com, sociologist Eric Kinenberg remarked, "I would argue that the rise of living alone represents the greatest social change of the last 60 years that we have failed to identify."[1]

3. We have garages.

Up through the early 1970s, most homes did not have garages. It seems inconsequential to our discussion on connections, but it isn't. If you live in a home with a garage today, you never have to speak to your neighbors. You can drive up, close the garage, and go into the house. This simple invention cut off the simple communication that occurred between neighbors when coming and going from home.

4. Technology has reduced communication to the lowest common denominator.

Much of our communication today, even with those closest to us, is not in person or even on the phone, but via email and text. And as you have probably experienced yourself, nuances can get lost in translation. There is a big difference between experiencing someone's voice, facial expressions, and body language and reading a text or email. Connection occurs on so many levels when you are able to communicate in person, or at least over the phone. For one, the communication is instant and sometimes even overlapping rather than communicating and then waiting for a response.

5. We express less.

"Good." "No." "Yep." "K." These are the typical responses I get when I text my college-age brother. While Twitter limits your messages to 140 characters or fewer, texts are often even shorter.

6. We have smaller support systems.

We have fewer friends, our families are smaller, and we are much less likely to live down the street from the people in our support network than ever before.

7. We are afraid to be vulnerable.

Authentic connection requires the kind of honesty and realness that allows another person to see you as human—as someone who feels. Whether what you feel is excitement or devastation, allowing another to see into your heart will open their heart to you and create connection, even if only for a moment. Hiding your emotions is a recipe for disconnection.

In her book *Alone Together: Why We Expect More from Technology and Less from Each Other*, Sherry Turkle discusses the impact of modern technology and how it has confused our perception of authentic connection. "Our networked life allows us to hide from each other," she says, "even as we are tethered to each other. We'd rather text than talk." So true. How many times have you stood in line or sat in the doctor's office or walked down the street and seen that there were more people staring at their smartphones than paying attention to the people and things around them? Some cities, Philadelphia and several college towns among them, have passed laws making it illegal to walk and text. Apparently we have become so obsessed with staying connected to what's going on "out there" that we have to be forced to pay attention to what's going on right in front of us, just so we don't get run over while crossing the street.

Today, for the first time in history, more adults are unmarried than married. And according to a Duke University study in 2006, Americans have fewer close friends or "confidants" today as they did in 1985—and the confidants are more likely to be someone they are related to. One quarter of the respondents said they had no one to confide in—double the number who said that in 1985.[2] We are also less likely to know our neighbors' names—and in my opinion, to care whether we know their names. Have the advances in technology, which have created higher expectations about how much we can accomplish in a day, caused us to have less time and energy for authentic connection? Even more so, do we value the need for authentic connection less because it has been replaced by the superficial communication of email, texting, and social media?

Connection Makes You Happy

So why does all this matter? Because other people matter in our lives. Social well-being is essential if you are going to be happy. Happy women are connected women. There are some simple ways to trigger your happiness through connection. Consider these:

1. Stop typing and start talking.

2. Make eye contact.

3. Tell the truth.

4. Get out of the house!

5. Put yourself around happy people.

Let's take a look at each of these.

Stop Typing and Start Talking

As technology has become central to how we communicate, it has become easier for us not to talk to anyone. Now, I admit, sometimes this is a good thing. When you want to check the balance on your credit card to see if a payment was received, you really might not want to talk to anyone. You just want the information. It is a transaction and it is easier to just let the automated system tell you your balance. But when your relationships become transactional in communication rather than interactional, there is a missed opportunity for connection. Have you ever had a text conversation like this?

How was ur day?

Good.

K. Just checkin.

Like the automated call to the bank, there are many times when being able to text or email or post on social media gives you a chance to communicate something when time would preclude you from making a phone call. The problem occurs when this becomes your exclusive mode of communication. As I talked to single women in particular, one of the most common complaints was that men—grown men over 30—often text them for dates or to say hello rather than calling. "It is a lazy way to communicate," said one of these women. "I thought it was unique to a couple of the men I have dated, but as I talk to my friends, they have all experienced the same frustration. How can you get to know someone when all you do is text?"

Technology allows you to communicate with more people in less depth, forming many loose connections but very few deep ones. If you want to be happy, you'll be better off logging off Facebook and opening up your black book. Next time you feel the urge to text that family member, try calling instead. Twice a day, instead of sending an email, pick up the phone and call your client or vendor—or walk over to your coworker's desk.

Make Eye Contact

If you want to connect, the quickest way to do so is to look the other person in the eye. Have you noticed lately? People seem more apt to walk by each other without looking at each other than they used to. Eye contact is an acknowledgment that the other person exists. Eye contact does more for connection than anything else. This is why people are can be more cruel online than they would be in person. Sure, your coworker might fire off an intimidating email, but if she has to sit down for a face-to-face conversation, the tone is typically milder.

Eye contact is linked directly to emotions. It is believed that the feel-good chemical oxytocin is released when we make eye contact. This is one reason that prolonged eye contact with someone we are not close to can feel awkward. It is also why eye contact is so important for couples, especially when they are trying to reconnect.

Tell the Truth: Vulnerability Is the Key to Real Connection

As a life coach, I have helped numerous clients who were struggling with how to tell someone something difficult. Perhaps they needed to say "no" to something they didn't want to do. For example, Suzanne sat in a session with me agonizing over telling her sister she no longer wanted to keep loaning her money.

"She has relied on me so much for so long. I finally understand that I am enabling her to not grow up and get her financial life together," she explained. "I feel guilty because I'm the one who finished college and got the good job. She dropped out after a year, and has never really landed on her feet with a career or anything. We were taught to look out for each other, so that's what I've done. But now I feel taken advantage of, like she feels entitled to my help. I have other goals and things I'd rather spend my money on, but I can't because she's always got a crisis of some sort—the car needs to be fixed, she's short coming up with the rent. She's getting too old for this!"

"Have you said this to your sister?" I asked.

"Well, not exactly," she replied.

"Why don't you tell her what you just told me? It's the truth about how you feel, right?" I said.

"I guess I've been afraid of hurting her feelings or putting a rift in our relationship," she admitted.

"Okay. Have you told your sister you are afraid to tell her how you feel because you're afraid of losing your relationship?" I asked.

She paused and thought about it. "No, I haven't said anything. I just get resentful and that shows up in how I interact with her sometimes. So the truth is, there is already a rift in the relationship," she said.

Suzanne mustered the courage to talk to her sister and tell her the truth she shared with me. "At first, she was defensive," Suzanne reported, "but I was sincere and I communicated with love, not anger. I even grabbed her hand at one point. I looked her in the eye the entire time. And when she became defensive, I noticed she wouldn't look me in the eye while talking. I asked her if she'd please turn toward me. That's when I noticed a shift. Finally she said, 'I hate that I'm like this. I'm thirty years old and I want to be able to make it on my own.'"

Suzanne was vulnerable enough to tell her sister the truth about how she was feeling—and to do so in love. The result was that Suzanne's vulnerability empowered her sister to be vulnerable enough to tell the truth too. It was a turning point in their relationship, and today, they have a healthier, happier relationship. It all began with a conversation that required them both to be vulnerable.

If you are going to connect authentically, you'll need to be vulnerable enough to be truthful—first with yourself, and then with others.

Get out of the House

On a recent Saturday I went with two friends to the Atlanta Jazz Festival—an annual event attended by about 150,000 people over three days. My girlfriends and I packed up snacks and drinks and blankets and found a spot in the sun on the vast lawn of Piedmont Park. As we chatted about everything from the weather to relationships to the people around us, it suddenly dawned on me. Although the huge stage and concert was supposed to be the center of the event, for us, it was nothing more than a backdrop to a conversation in the sun—in the midst of thousands of people. I looked around and we weren't the only ones who could be described this way. Most were paying no attention to the music, except when it stopped and everyone clapped. Instead, they were buzzing about in various conversations. Kids were playing. Adults were laughing and talking. A few people threw Frisbees and footballs.

"Do you think people just want to be among people?" I said to one friend. "Because it doesn't appear that any of us are doing anything we couldn't have stayed home to do in our own backyards or living rooms." Somehow, though, going somewhere and being connected with others multiplied the energy of the afternoon. So even in a big crowd at a festival, connection can occur because we feel a part of something bigger—a sense of connection to our community.

Be Around Happy People

Did you know happiness is contagious? Having happy people in your network of friends and family makes it more likely you'll be happy. Apparently, birds of a feather do indeed flock together. So just by doing some of the things in this book, you might just influence the happiness of those around you. People with the most social connections— whether a spouse, friends, neighbors, coworkers, or relatives—are happier. And every additional happy person in your network positively impacts your own happiness, according to researchers at Harvard Medical School.[3] Using information from the famous Framingham Heart Study, which showed that ills such as smoking and obesity are spread within networks, it was determined that positive outcomes such as happiness also spread within networks. If one of your close social connections is happy, the likelihood you are happy increases by 15 percent! Even more surprising, if a friend of one of your social connections is happy, your chances for happiness increase by 10 percent. Each unhappy friend increases your chances for being unhappy by 7 percent. To compare that with the impact of money on your happiness, researchers conclude that a happy friend increases your happiness by the same amount as having an extra $20,000.

Of course, sometimes our friends and family members are unhappy for good reason. They are going through a difficult time, for example. But when you consider new friends or a potential mate, choose wisely and carefully. Their happiness habits will affect your own. When you are feeling down, be intentional about spending time around your happy friends. They are sure to lift your spirits. Think about the people within your network, from your spouse and children to siblings, parents, other relatives, friends, neighbors, and colleagues. Who are the happy people among your social connections? Do you spend more time with happy people or unhappy people?

Connection Keeps You Grounded

While in the thick of writing this book lessons seem to appear constantly. Last Wednesday, I was still on a high from my trip to New York. It had included an appearance on the *Today* show and quick meetings with several other media outlets. It was a fun, productive dream of a trip. But it had been impromptu, and I hadn't planned on being out the first two days of the week. People often assume I don't have time for anything other than work. In reality, I am committed to making sure my life is about much more than work. If it wasn't, I don't think I'd have much inspiration to share with you. But I must admit, it takes a lot of intentionality to keep a sense of balance between my personal and professional life, especially when work isn't always predictable and deadlines are real. I'm much better at it than I used to be.

I don't know all you have going on, but I bet you can relate! Whether it's your employer expecting you to do more with less, taking care of loved ones, or just trying to figure out when you can squeeze in a workout, it's a challenge getting it all done with grace. Shoot. It's a challenge getting it all done, period.

Each night, I keep a really brief journal—two to three sentences that sum up the most significant moments of that day. It takes about 60 seconds. And it gives me a sense of clarity about what really matters. For example, last Wednesday after getting back from my trip, what I wrote in my journal wasn't about all the phone calls and emails from friends and family about my television appearance. Instead, it was my excitement over the delivery of a new patio swing for my backyard and meeting one of my best friends, Yvette, at Pier 1 to pick out seat pillows for the swing. When I arrived in the parking lot to meet her, I had emerged just five minutes earlier from a massage that calmed me down from the adrenaline rush of the previous two days. Yvette was wiped out from back-to-back meetings at her job—so much so that she arrived in the parking lot early enough to take a nap. I parked. She got out. And we walked like two old ladies on a leisurely stroll. When it occurred to us how slow we were walking, we looked at each other and cracked up.

"It's been quite a week already, huh?" I said.

"Yeah," was all she managed to respond.

We walked in and spent the next 30 minutes deliberating over the benefits of patterns versus solids, neutrals versus brights. It was fun. And a break.

Why did picking out pillows for the swing matter most of all that day? Because when I think of swinging, I think of my great-grandmother's front porch in South Carolina when I was a kid. I think of sitting on the porch swing with my cousins, chatting with aunties and uncles, hearing stories about my grandmother pouring sugar down the well on the side of the house to secretly make sugar water (and the subsequent spanking she got!). I also think of the swing set in my backyard as a little girl on Tyndall Air Force Base in Florida. I would swing for what seemed like hours, looking at the dolphins jumping and playing in the Gulf of Mexico behind our house. I wasn't looking for a swing, but when I saw one the other week while shopping, it immediately felt right to get it.

When Yvette and I got to my house, we headed straight to the back patio to tie on the seat pillows. They fit perfectly! We decided to take a swing. Feet dangling and gazing at the trees in front of us, we enjoyed a simple moment of doing nothing.

My point? In the midst of a hectic pace and professional successes, the stuff that holds the most meaning to you is usually connected to people you love and the joyful experiences you've had. As you move to higher levels of success, it is even more important to stay grounded in the simple experiences of life that hold special meaning for you. Don't take a moment with a friend for granted. Or dinner tonight with your family. Or that phone call you've been meaning to make. All the professional and financial success in the world means little if you don't have a meaningful, connected life outside of work.

Activate This Happiness Trigger!

- Get at least six hours of social time each day. This can include any activity in which you are interacting with others, including work, phone calls, and meals.

- Tell the truth. In a conversation you need to have, what would happen if you were simply honest and told the truth?

- Take off the mask and be vulnerable. Being vulnerable means being honest about who you are and what you feel. When connecting with others, vulnerability is key.

- Get around someone happy! One of the quickest ways to practice the habit of being happy is to be around others who make a habit of being happy.

- Make eye contact.

- In your close relationships, hug, smile, hold hands, touch!

CONVERSATION STARTER:

Spread the Happiness

It's time for a happiness movement

Points to Ponder

- The pressure to appear happy often leads women to put on a game face. We're not talking with each other, which means we aren't sharing solutions with each other either.

- Change of any sort usually begins person to person, one convert at a time.

- You have the power to foster more happiness among the women you know. Just start the conversation.

Conversation Starters

- Happiness is contagious. Are you spreading it? If not, what are you spreading?

- Who are the women in your circle of influence you'd enjoy serving with and supporting as you all move toward greater happiness in your lives?

- What could you and your friends do to be of service in your community?

The cultural shifts over the last 40 years are stealing women's happiness—and it's so subtle that we don't even notice. But we can do something about it, and it begins with women who are willing to speak up and start talking about what it takes to be happy—and what it doesn't. I believe you can be one of those leaders to help start a happiness movement. Whether you start with your sister, your girlfriend, your daughter, your mom, or your entire neighborhood or church, I want to give you some tools to get the conversation going.

It's very simple. It doesn't cost a thing. What I want is for you to use the conversation of women and happiness to connect and start the conversation. By opening up the discussion, you will empower the women around you to be authentic about the real challenges and wins they are experiencing in everyday life. Most importantly, you'll help them understand the ways they can trigger greater happiness every day.

The tools are online. Go to www.valorieburton.com/girlfriends so you can download a free Girlfriends' Gab Guide. It includes a leader guide for you and any others who will help, ideas for get-togethers, a video to get the conversation going, and a girlfriends' "happiness trigger" cheat sheet with tips on activating each of the 13 happiness triggers!

Connection is about heart-to-heart communication. And what better way to have it than with a group of like-minded women, all getting together with the sole goal of becoming happier? Take a few simple steps:

1. **Decide to make a difference by** kindling the conversation between women in your social circle. It's easy. And as women, we don't talk enough about what's really going on and the simple things we can do to be happier.

2. **Choose a date and time** for your girlfriends' get-together. Whether you want to get the women at work together at lunchtime or host a literal "Happy Hour" of chatting about what it takes to be happy, plan a get-together that facilitates connection and open conversation. Schedule a girls' night in and have salad and pizza or an afternoon ice cream social (my personal favorite)!

3. **Invite them and they will come!** You can evite, call, text, or send invitations. Make it easy on yourself and make it easy for people to respond. It doesn't need to be formal, unless that's your style.

4. **Start the conversation with the Girlfriends' Gab Guide!**
   Download and use the guide at www.valorieburton.com/
   girlfriends and use the questions to spark conversation about
   cultural shifts, real-life challenges, and how to use the happiness
   triggers to boost your happiness. Encourage your friends to get
   a book of their own, try the happiness triggers, and become a
   part of the happiness movement.

5. **Let me know how it goes!** I guarantee this get-together will
   ignite passionate discussion and ideas among the women in
   your life. I know it did when I hosted my own Girlfriends' Get-
   Together using the very questions I share in the Girlfriends'
   Gab Guide. If you've decided to engage in social media, tweet
   me or Facebook me to let me know how your get-together goes!
   Twitter @valorieburton and Facebook www.facebook.com/
   valorieburtonfanpage.

Flow

*How to disrupt your distractions and make
the pressure of time disappear*

Decision:

"I minimize interruptions so I can fully engage in the activity at hand."

We so often fly by the seat of our pants. Have you ever noticed that feeling? It is as though you are just trying to get stuff done. You don't get to actually do anything with your full attention, giving it the excellence it deserves or the time you deserve. Instead, you race from one activity to the next, sometimes barely making it, and with an ever-present awareness of the next thing calling from your to-do list. It makes you stressed, not happy.

One of the most elusive happiness triggers is flow—your ability to concentrate so intently on an activity that you become absolutely absorbed in it. According to researcher Dr. Mihaly Csikszentmihalyi, author of *Flow: The Psychology of the Optimal Experience*, we all experience flow and we feel similar characteristics when we are in flow. You feel alive and alert. You are not self-conscious. You feel a deep satisfaction with your efforts, and your efforts may even feel "effortless." You are in flow, at your best. Athletes and performers often describe flow as being "in the zone." Writers and artists will say they feel like the work was flowing through them, almost effortlessly, as though they couldn't get it out fast enough.

But flow doesn't just happen in the realm of sports and entertainment and art. It can happen even if your work does not fall into one of these categories. The store clerk who so enjoys helping customers that she loses track of the time and says, "Is it time to go already?" is in flow. So too is the schoolteacher who gets lost in the excitement of teaching new material—so much so that her students have an enthusiasm unseen in their other classes. Suddenly they love math, even though last year they thought they hated it! Her passion and flow become contagious and inspire and elevate the students.

Flow is increasingly difficult for women (and men, for that matter!) in today's culture. We live in an age of interruption. When was the last time you were able to do anything uninterrupted? Can't remember? Join the club. We are wired to be constantly interrupted. If it isn't your cell phone ringing, it's the text message that just came in or the telemarketer calling your home phone or the email chime alerting you to your latest message, which may actually be spam, but hey, at least now you know it's there waiting to be read. However, technology isn't the only culprit. If you are a mom, especially a mom of young children, the idea of doing anything with full concentration when your children are around—other than take care of your children—is pretty much impossible. At work, you are often expected to be on call, responding to the needs of whoever has a question, wants something done, or just wants to chat.

But let's not kid ourselves. Often, even when we have a moment to become fully engaged with what we are doing, we don't need technology or people to distract us. We can be pretty good at distracting ourselves! Ever notice how much you get done when you are supposed to be doing something else? Procrastination is the master stealer of your ability to be in flow.

If you have too much on your to-do list, you'll find that flow is a rare achievement for you. It is the curse of overload, overdrive, and overwhelm. Even if everything on your schedule is stuff you actually want to do, when there's too much of it, you don't get to enjoy it. And this steals your happiness. I always know I am at that point when I become stressed about something like driving home two hours to see my family or flying to a speaking engagement. These are things I thoroughly enjoy. I am relaxed doing them. I am in flow, smiling, feeling perfectly in the right place. The exception comes when I try to cram too much into a day or week. Then I'm not in flow, smiling, or feeling perfectly in the right place. Have you been there?

What Makes Time Fly for You?

When I was a child, I would beg my mother to drop me off at the library. I didn't really want her to go with me because for me, the world of books was an adventure. There was no telling what I might find on the next shelf! I didn't want to be limited by time or a schedule. I wanted to get lost in the world of books—a never-ending abundance of stories and information. I didn't realize it then, but I was in flow when I was at the library.

When you're truly in flow, you will accomplish and do things that others might find odd or simply would have no interest in doing. Case in point. During the summer between third and fourth grade, the librarians on the base where we were stationed encouraged me to enter a reading contest. I won. I still have my grand prize: a full color world encyclopedia. I thought, "More stuff to read! Yippee!" The thing is, I didn't just win by a little. I read almost three times as many books (64 in total) as the second place winner (23). And no one pushed me to do it. I was having fun. That summer, I joined Harriet Tubman on the Underground Railroad and Cassius Clay as he transformed into Muhammad Ali. I learned the answer to the question, "Are you there God? It's me, Margaret" and made a bunch of barnyard friends in *Charlotte's Web*. More than three decades later, I still remember how much I enjoyed the book reading challenge that summer. It made me happy. Still does. Drop me off at the local bookstore on a day when I have time. I never get bored. I just move from section to section, exploring the latest fun novels, self-help, Christian inspiration, and biographies. No wonder I'm an author. Books are my flow, whether reading them or writing them.

A friend pointed out to me one day that books grace every room in my house. They lie decoratively on tables, waiting to be picked up again, inviting new readers to flip through their pages. It happened organically. I don't recall ever saying to myself, "Valorie, you should have books in every room." I didn't have to. I have a relationship with my books. Some of them helped me gain a new perspective or gave me hope when I needed it. Others made me laugh or accompanied me at the beach, keeping me entertained as I soaked up the sun and sounds of waves crashing on shore. Still others took me on trips through history and allowed me to get up close and personal with fascinating people.

What's your flow? What is it that you do that allows time to fly by?

What leads you into a state of flow is likely different from what does it for me. Think back to an activity you were engaged in, in which time seemed to just fly by. If you can think of more than one, great! List them all.

_____

_____

_____

_____

What's Distracting You?

The biggest problem with getting in flow are interruptions that distract us from what we want to focus on. Research shows that interruptions decrease your happiness. One potential reason is that it disrupts flow and also leaves you feeling less in control. Be intentional about sizing up your distractions and make a plan to eliminate them one by one. For example, if you want to fully engage with a project at work, make a list of what happened that last time you sat down to engage in such a project and found yourself continually distracted. It may take some discipline on your part. For example, you might need to log out of your Internet connection altogether to keep you from succumbing to the temptation to surf the web. You might need to turn your cell phone on airplane mode so that rather than seeing that someone's calling and needing to be disciplined enough not to answer, you don't get the call at all. Besides, any distraction that you have to ignore is still a distraction.

It takes energy to be disciplined, so eliminate the need to be disciplined by stopping distractions before they appear. When the phone rings, even if you ignore it, you will probably ask yourself, "I wonder why she was calling? Oh yeah, I told her I'd send her the link to the website yesterday and I forgot…Well, it'll only take a moment so let me do that right quick." You know how it goes. It is a slippery slope and your best bet is to stay focused. If there are people on your list of distractions, talk to them before you attempt to have focused time. That way, you won't have to explain it while you are trying to concentrate. If there is something about your environment that distracts you—loud noise or clutter, for example—address that too. For example, when I am focused at my desk, I often use white noise from an app on my phone called SleepStream. There are usually people working and talking in the offices outside my door and the white noise keeps me from hearing their conversations as well as the ticking clock in my office. It works for me. Find what works for you.

Throw Yourself into What You're Doing

While speaking at an event in Kansas City, a high school graduate who was being honored with a scholarship described her philosophy on why she applied to only one college—a prestigious arts college in New York. "They told me, 'Don't put all your eggs in one basket!'" she said. Then she explained, "But I like this basket!" The audience laughed. I loved the boldness and clarity in her statement.

In a culture that often advises you to have a backup plan just in case your dreams don't work out, it is counterintuitive to put all your eggs in one basket. But in planning for the "just in case" scenario, sometimes you spread yourself too thin and don't put enough energy (eggs) into the one dream (basket) you really want. Take a look at where you are focusing your energy. Is it mostly on moving in the direction of your vision? Or are you spread so thin there are few resources or energy left for the goals you really want to manifest?

Too many baskets can water down your efforts and keep you from engaging in any one endeavor. It is often fear that keeps you from committing yourself fully to the thing you most want. Whether it is a relationship, a job, or a business venture, anything worth having is worth giving your all. In the event that you put all your eggs in one basket and that basket is lost, trust that you have the ability and faith to use the wisdom gained to rebuild and start again. You are resilient. And if you have to start over, you can do it.

This example is a wider view of what it means to be in flow, but it is so relevant to the conversation on happiness for us as women. Too often, we behave as though this life is a trial run. It is as though we believe that someday we'll get a chance to come back and do it just as we wanted to. Not so. Throw yourself fully into the opportunity in front of you and you may just be surprised at how more opportunities and joy begin to flow to you. It is difficult to throw yourself fully into one opportunity when you are simultaneously pursuing three others. One of my favorite sayings is this: "He who chases two rabbits will catch neither."

Helping Others Get in Flow

Ideas for using this trigger with people who have this as a signature trigger:

- Notice what activities seem to make them light up. What are they doing when you see their energy immediately shift higher? Plan an activity or project around what energizes them.

- Recognize that their best performance will come when the challenge before them is at just the right level—not so far above their skills that they become frustrated and not so easy they become bored. If you are in a leadership role with the person (as a boss or parent, for example), this means being intentional about what you ask of them.

- Be careful about loading their schedule with too many unrelated activities. Clear blocks of uninterrupted time.

- Give them the space to get in the flow. Need to ask a question while they are in flow? Unless it's an emergency, let it wait!

Activate This Happiness Trigger!

- Don't spread yourself so thin there are no resources or energy to focus on what matters most! Concentrate your efforts. Don't be afraid to throw yourself into what you really want. Put your eggs in one basket!

- Ask yourself this: In what way are you spreading yourself too thin? What goal do you need to put more energy or resources into? What will you have to let go of in order to find the additional energy or resources to dedicate to your goal?

- Identify the top three distractions that are stealing your focus right now. Ask, how could I eliminate (or at least dramatically minimize) each of these distractions?

- What activity leads you into a state of flow? Can you engage in it right now? Go for it!

- Identify the top three distractions that keep you from being able to focus at work and get to your priorities. Come up with a solution for eliminating, or at least minimizing, those distractions.

- When sitting down for a meal, whether alone or with others, put your cell phone away, do not answer landline calls, turn off the television, and be fully present.

- Identify your strengths and use them at work. If you are unable to find ways to use your strengths, set a goal and deadline to land work you love. Refuse to settle for spending 2,080 plus hours per year doing work that bores you and doesn't allow you to contribute the best of who you are.

- Make a list of activities that, when you engage in them, make you lose track of time. Engage in at least one of these activities each day. Here are a few examples to get you started: Doing work you love, playing with your kids, engaging in a favorite hobby, getting lost in books at your local bookstore, spending time with your loved ones, fill in the blank _____.

Confessions of a Recovering Procrastinator

*How perfectionism makes you think
you're busier than you are*

Points to Ponder

- The modern rewards of instant gratification (texts, emails, instant messaging, Skype) make it easier than ever to get distracted.

- Perfectionism is your enemy and it often manifests as procrastination. You won't get started because you don't have it all figured out yet. Sound familiar?

- Procrastination causes unnecessary anxiety that zaps your happiness.

Conversation Starters

- When are you most likely to procrastinate?

- What gets you unstuck?

- Why do you feel you must do things perfectly? What would happen if you didn't?

I'm writing this from my hotel room. One mile from home. I know. It's strange. I tried to explain it to a good friend who called:

"I'm at a hotel down the street," I said.

"What city are you in?"

"Atlanta."

"You mean, you're going home to Atlanta tomorrow?" she asked.

"No, I'm at a hotel in Atlanta."

"Oh," said my friend. "So you are speaking in Atlanta tomorrow and you're staying in the hotel where you have a speaking engagement tomorrow?"

"No," I said. "I don't have a speaking engagement tomorrow. I just decided to stay down the street from home at a hotel."

Silence.

"So…" my friend said. "How much is that costing you?"

Okay, here's the deal. I looked at everything that I needed to accomplish before closing up shop for the holidays and decided as "a recovering procrastinator with a tendency to relapse," I had better come up with a plan to help me focus. So I checked myself in to a hotel, which gave me an undistracted environment with a focused agenda—not to mention the threat of wasting my money if I check out without finishing what I checked in to do. I found myself energized and productive.

When I get stuck, sometimes all I need is a change of environment. How about you? Perhaps a new environment could be just the boost you need to be productive or start envisioning what you want to do in the coming week or year. Whether an afternoon at Starbucks or a weekend away, breaking out of your comfort zone physically can help you break out of your comfort zone mentally.

Play

*Why women play less than men, and why you
should start having more fun right now*

Decision:

"I give myself permission to play, be silly, and have fun!"

I t was my third time around the lazy river pool at the Orlando resort where I'd spoken two days earlier. I just love when a speaking engagement takes me somewhere worth staying after I'm done working. I'm not a particularly good swimmer so meandering on the fully inflated blue donut along the curves of the pool and under the waterfalls suited me just fine. As my feet splashed in the water and I relaxed in the sun, the sound of children's voices and adults' laughter left me feeling relaxed and happy. Sometime around the third lap, though, I began itching for a bigger adventure.

That's when I noticed the kids on the other side of the pool area yelling with elation as they jetted down a long, winding waterslide, landing with a big splash at the other side of the pool. "How fun," I thought as I remembered how much fun my friends and I used to have at the water park in Denver when I was a tween. The whole way down I would anticipate what the splash was going to be like, how far down in the water I'd land, whether I'd held my breath the right way to keep the water from going up my nose, and the sheer joy of the crash into the water at the end. As my speed accelerated, I would sometimes try to slow myself down, but it was no use. Once you head down the slide, you are no longer in control. So you might as well let go and enjoy the ride!

As I snapped out of my childhood flashback and remembered I was in the pool in Orlando, it dawned on me: Get on the slide! There's no age limit. Do it. I climbed out of the lazy river pool and walked over to the pool with the slide. The two workers manning the slide barely noticed. For some reason, my inner doubting voice that sometimes imagines what other people are thinking feared they might ask for my ID or check to see if I was too tall, like they do for the playroom at fast food restaurants. "You can't get on the waterslide!" I was expecting them to say. "You know you're too big for this! This is for kids. You're lucky we let you in the lazy river." But no one said a word. I sat at the top of the slide and inched to the edge…and then I slipped down the slide, giddy and giggling all the way down.

I landed and went under. Now my hair was completely wet (something I was able to avoid on the float!). "Might as well do it again!" I thought. But this time I was more confident. As I inched to the edge at the top of the slide, I lifted my hands above my head. Big mistake. The same giddy sensation overcame me as I slipped down the slide and landed with a big splash in the pool. As I emerged from the pool, the two workers manning the booth seemed to be laughing and excited too, and maybe a little embarrassed? Their eyes were wide as they watched me pop up out of the water after going under. To my horror, I suddenly realized I'd had a brief wardrobe malfunction on the way down the slide! I looked around to see who else might have noticed. Whew. Nobody. Or at least no one acted as though they saw anything.

To avoid another mishap, I figured two trips down the waterslide had been enough and headed to my poolside lounge chair. "Back to my reading," I decided. Maybe it was time to engage in the happiness trigger of relaxation. Enough play for one day.

> "It is a happy talent to know how to play." —*Ralph Waldo Emerson*

"Play" isn't something we talk about a lot as women, but we should. Or rather we should just do it. It seems men play more. Even grown men commonly shoot hoops together or join the softball league. They get out on the golf course and even play video games. When you think of "horsing around," you typically think of boys and men, not girls and women. But studies show play is important to your well-being in many ways—one of which is experiencing more happiness in your life. In fact, a study led by Dr. Alan Krueger of Princeton University found that we are happiest when we are engaging in leisure activities.[1] But in a world that over-focuses on work and productivity, play is far down the to-do list of most women, if it makes the to-do list at all.

Psychologists have long noticed that boys and men often bond side by side as they play. Whether wrestling as boys (something you rarely see girls do!) or playing a game of pickup basketball or competing side by side with video games, it seems a natural way for men to connect. Women, on the other hand, tend to bond face-to-face. We want to talk, listen, and share. The more we feel heard, the easier it is to bond. That doesn't mean, however, that we should skip play. It might be more important in this day and age than ever because play gives your mind a break. When fully engaged in it, you are absorbed in what you are doing and able to momentarily forget all of your other cares. You can't play and multitask.

In today's culture, we have become almost obsessed with work and producing results for everything we do. But play is not about results. The value is in the experience. Play reduces stress and unleashes creativity as you engage in an activity purely for the joy and interest of it.

Why Play Makes You Happier

Play may actually reveal even more of your character than work. We choose ways to play based on what intrinsically interests and drives us, whereas work choices are not always based on what we most want to be doing at any given moment. What play looks like to you may not resonate with me—and vice versa. So you can learn a great deal about a woman by what activities she chooses to engage in as play. Likewise, you can learn a lot by *whether* she chooses to engage in play at all. Here's what makes play a happiness trigger. It does the following:

- It gives your mind a break by taking you out of the stressful world of productivity and results and into a world of experience for the sake of experience.

- Play gives you an outlet of personal expression.
- When done with others, play promotes authentic connection and bonding.
- It frees your mind to let go of the stress of everyday problems and lets you focus entirely on the activity at hand.
- It can reconnect you with the core of who you are—your gifts, passion, and talents.
- Play is fun!

Types of Play

The National Institute for Play, founded by play researcher Dr. Stuart Brown, describes what it calls seven "patterns of play."[2] You may find this helpful as you find ways to incorporate more play into your life.

Attunement Play

These are playful interactions, such as the ones experienced between a mother and her infant. The mother makes eye contact with the baby, and the baby responds with a smile. The mother smiles back, the baby coos. There is a rhythm that takes place and imaging technology would show that the right cerebral cortex is "attuned" in the baby's brain as well as the mother's.

Body Play and Movement

Leaping, dancing, and movement of all sorts is a form of play. It stimulates the brain and facilitates learning.

Object Play

This is about using objects as the focus of play. It tends to pique curiosity. Whether a girl playing with her baby doll or Double Dutch with her friends or an adult playing pool or making jewelry for fun, object play helps brain development.

Social Play

From wrestling and tickling to the back-and-forth of a fun conversation, social play is about communicating and belonging.

Imaginative and Pretend Play

Kids are great at make-believe. They can play for hours making up stories with their toy characters. Having the ability to imagine can take you far as an adult as you envision possibilities, play with your children, or give yourself permission to sing your heart out at karaoke, pretending you're a superstar.

Storytelling/Narrative Play

In early childhood, storytelling is a key tool for learning and understanding the world and how it works. But telling stories and developing a narrative about your life, especially one that includes the humorous side, can be a powerful form of play.

Creative Play

I call this one freestyle play. Whether using your creativity to play music, paint, shoot photography, or play games, creative play allows you to step out of the ordinary.

Learning to Play

I wish I could say play was my strong suit. I love it, but I have to remember to do it. Otherwise, my serious side takes over. I even have a dry sense of humor—so much so that it isn't unusual for people not to realize that I'm joking. I remember my parents' utter excitement once at the sight of me skipping across a hotel room when I was about seven years old. I'm not sure what made me skip—I think I may have been excited about moving to Germany. We had just gotten there and didn't even have our housing yet, hence the hotel room. When I skipped spontaneously across the room, they both looked at each other with surprise, as if to say, "Look, she really *is* a kid! She skips! That's proof right there." They made such a big deal out of it that I thought maybe I should skip every once and a while just to reassure them.

Their surprise was well-founded. My mother loves to tell the story about how when I was five and we went to Disney World with family and friends, I was the only kid who didn't get excited when Mickey Mouse and his friends walked by. Apparently, all the other children started jumping up and down and yelling, "Mommy, it's Mickey Mouse! Donald Duck! Daddy, look!" I, on the other hand, was not buying it. "That's not Mickey," I said, sounding wise to Disney's attempt to fool me with Mickey and friends impersonators. "Look at Mickey's legs! Those are *people legs*!" I said to my mother. "That's not the real Mickey!" I was enough of a kid to still believe Mickey was a living being, but that Disney character in front of me? *He was fake.*

Overthinking. Now, that will get in the way of your ability to play.

Some of us play naturally and others of us have to learn to do it. In fact, if you're a mom, I encourage you to let your children play. Cheer them on. Play along with them. Lead by example by letting them see you have fun and be silly sometimes. Rather than taking everything too seriously, joke with them. Laugh at yourself when you make mistakes. Let them see your playful side. And consider getting them involved in a team sport or group play at some point where they can learn to play with others.

Do Something That Makes You Happy (You Don't Have to Be Good at It)

The best thing about authentic play is that it's not about being good. It's about having fun. It is about the experience. So go ahead. Start painting. Nobody said you have to be Picasso. Paint badly. And have fun!

Can't make the church choir, but love to sing? Don't stifle yourself. Sing! Sing loudly. Enjoy it. Have fun.

Don't have any rhythm, but love to dance? That's fine too. Dance your heart out! Express yourself.

Play is about expression, not judgment. Research shows that play through self-expression, such as singing, can have health benefits. A 1998 study showed that nursing home residents who participated in a singing program for a month experienced decreases in anxiety as well as depression. Singing can have similar psychological effects as exercise, such as releasing endorphins and increasing blood circulation, which also improves your mood.

In fact, the six most happiness-inducing activities, according to London School of Economics researcher George MacKerron, are:

1. Making love

2. Sports and exercise

3. Theater/dance/concerts

4. Singing and performing

5. Exhibitions/museum/library

6. Hobbies/arts/crafts

MacKerron's research used an iPhone app that randomly dinged two times each day and had participants take a short survey on their happiness and alertness. The study includes more than three million data points and 45,000 participants. Those who responded during or immediately following an activity were noticeably happier than those who were not engaged in an activity. Whether or not they were particularly good at the activity was irrelevant. The fact that they were engaged in the activity is the point.

I play tennis. I'm awful at it, but I love it. In my life, I've had only three tennis partners—all equally as bad as I am. That way, we can have fun and nobody gets frustrated. My first partner, Mike, was a fellow cadet during my first year of college when I was at the US Air Force Academy. I was thrust onto the tennis team after a brief (three week) stint playing hooker (I know, not the best title, but it's the position of "forward") on the women's rugby team. It was probably a good thing I left the team because they won the NCAA Championship that year, and somehow, I don't think they would have done it with the 5 foot 1 inch 110-pound never-played-a-sport-involving-a-ball Cadet Burton on the team. I didn't have a clue what I was doing and didn't enjoy getting tackled, but the camaraderie was great.

Anyway, I moved on. At the Academy, you had to play a sport and

Mike and I were assigned to the intramural tennis team. Neither of us had ever taken a lesson—and it was obvious. We had fun, though. And we frustrated the dickens out of the other doubles players who wanted a good match. Unfortunately, they were not going to get it with us.

Fast-forward seven years. I took lessons and met a new friend in my tennis class named Margaret. We played each other and only each other—too merciful to subject any of our tennis-playing friends to our novice skills. She was in public relations, like I was at the time. And we had good conversations in between serves—and we had a good excuse to wear really cute tennis outfits. (I think it is perfectly okay to choose your sport based on the outfits. Fun outfits empower you to have more fun. No research on that theory, just personal speculation.)

Years later, I picked up tennis again and played with my friend and neighbor Cheryl. We liked to play on the court down the street, a short walking distance from home. I started to get a little better, but honestly, I never wanted to play tennis because I wanted to win a tennis match. I don't even expect to "win" and I don't care. I don't practice, I just play. I genuinely enjoy running around the court trying to hit the ball. I give myself permission to never be all that good at it. And that's just fine with me. I have plenty of things that I find important to be good at it, but it's nice to have something in which there is no pressure to perform, to win, to look graceful. The sole goal is to enjoy myself.

How about you? What would you play if you didn't have to be "good" at it? Whether it's art or music or a sport, play for the fun of it.

What's Your Hobby?

One of the easiest ways to incorporate play into your everyday life is to have a hobby. Do you have one? When is the last time you engaged in it? I love making jewelry and doing makeup. Very girly hobbies, I know. But that's what I like. I figured out one day that I love putting on makeup—especially when I can take my time. I have tons of makeup. I buy books by makeup artists and I am fascinated by what they do. I first learned to do makeup modeling while doing pageants as a teenager. I loved it then and while I am certainly no teenager today, I am still quite happy playing with makeup. I believe it is a form of art, like painting or drawing. It just happens that the canvas is you.

So on a day when I have time, I'll play. I try new colors. I follow along with the directions in one of my makeup artist books. And when I'm done, I might wash it all off. I'm just doing it for fun. Your hobby can be uniquely your own, as long as it engages you, brings you joy, and doesn't become "work."

Work as Play

In light of my earlier suggestion that, particularly in our culture, the idea of play often gets devalued because it's not "producing" something, suggesting work as play may seem counterintuitive. However, there are those for whom work really is play. They so love what they do, they'd do it for free. A friend who started a successful clothing line in the 1990s used to describe his work all the time as play. "I don't work," he told me. "I play." This is not to say there aren't deadlines and stress, but when the core of the activity you perform at work feels like play to you, it will transform your life.

According to research by Gallup, those with high career well-being, in which they are able to engage their strengths every day, are twice as likely to have high well-being in their overall lives. So if work isn't play and you want to continue working, I encourage you to ponder that thought. How could your work feel like play? What would you have to do differently?

Activate This Happiness Trigger!

- Give yourself permission to play at something you're no good at, just because you like doing it. Sing, dance, play the guitar, take up golf! Do it for pure pleasure.

- Prioritize time to play. Value the "experience" of play without the pressure of needing to produce results or be productive.

- Loosen up and be playful—in conversation, in relation-ships, and in life.

- Engage in a hobby regularly. If you don't have one, explore one.

6 Types of Friends You Need

Points to Ponder

- Studies show that it is a good idea to have several types of friends rather than relying on one or two to meet all of your needs.

- Statistically speaking, your relationship with your girlfriends will likely outlast your marriage, your parents, and your coworkers.

- One study showed that when fewer than 15 percent of the women in a firm were in positions of power, the women were competitive and backstabbing with each other. But when women represented more than 15 percent of the powerful positions, women were collaborative.

Conversation Starter

- Do you rely on just one good friend? What would it take to nurture a few more close friendships?

- Why do you think some women are competitive with other women, but not the men?

- What can you do to put other women at ease and facilitate more authentic connections with women in your circle of influence?

Do You Have the Right Mix of Friends?

Not every friend can meet every need. Some will meet more than one need, but few can do it all! Here are six types of friends every woman needs:

The Wise Friend. You can count on her to talk you out of doing something you'd regret, help you solve your latest dilemma, and give all-around sound advice about just about anything.

The Fun Friend. Want to have a good time, be adventurous, or laugh til your stomach hurts? You can always count on this one.

The Travel Buddy. Drama-free, this friend is adaptable, maybe even adventurous, and loves to see the world.

The Relationship Coach. Transparent, real, and willing to listen, this friend has figured a few things out in the love department and genuinely wants to see you happy when it comes to romance.

The Career Comrade. You share a similar background and goals in your work life and encourage each other to higher professional success.

The Accountability Partner. To maximize your potential, this is your go-to pal to help keep you on track.

Now, let's turn the tables. Think of your four closest friends. Which type of friend are you to each of them?

Relaxation

Why women worry more than men...
and what you can do about it

Decision:

"I sleep. I rest. I embrace what is."

It was the night before my father's corrective open heart surgery. I was staying at my dad's so I could drive him to the hospital early the next morning. During a routine physical several weeks earlier, doctors had discovered some irregularity in my father's heartbeat and sent him for further testing, which revealed that although his arteries were "in perfect condition," one of them was wired wrong. It was going to the wrong place! Amazed by his longevity, he was told that his rare condition should have taken his life when he was a young child. The fact that he'd played sports as a kid and served nearly a quarter century in the military was a miracle. To give him a better chance at a longer life expectancy, he'd need surgery to fix the problem.

They gave us a DVD on the procedure and I watched it carefully on the eve of his surgery. It scared the heck out of me! They'd need to stop my father's heart and cut through his sternum with a specially-made saw to perform the procedure. As a responsible daughter, it had seemed like a smart idea to watch the video. In reality, it had caused me more worry than good.

I left my room and went into the living room to see how my dad was feeling.

"Hey, Dad," I said, trying to sound perfectly relaxed. "How are you feeling about everything?"

"Well, like I told you before," he said in a matter-of-fact tone, "I don't think God brought me this far with a heart defect just to take me when the doctors discover it and get ready to fix it."

"Now, you do understand what they are going to do tomorrow, right?" I said, thinking about the seriousness of the surgery I'd just learned about on the video.

"Yeah, yeah, I do" he said.

"Well, I just watched the video. Did you know they are going to stop your heart and cut through your…" I started.

"I know, I know," he said, cutting me off in mid-sentence. "I don't need to think about all that. All I know is the surgery is going to go fine."

With that, I stopped my questioning and went to bed. He was calm. I was not. I'd been imagining worst-case scenarios for the three weeks since we were told he needed surgery. He didn't know it, but I'd reminisced about all the great conversations my dad and I had had. I pondered the possibility we might not have any more of them. I imagined how I would respond if the surgery failed. I wondered how on earth doctors could stop a person's heart and get it pumping again. I imagined the doctors forgetting a key step or doing something wrong.

You get the picture. My imagination got the best of me. I was worried. Dad was not.

Women Worry More

Research shows that as women, we worry more than men—even in the same situation.[1] And worry is bound to impact your happiness.

Men compartmentalize. They can get into an argument in the morning and focus completely on work during the day, solving the argument when they get off work. Not true for many women. An argument in the morning will throw off the whole day. And don't let a couple get into a contentious conversation in the evening. Her husband says, "Let's finish this tomorrow," while his wife will want to keep talking until the issue is resolved. "How can I go to sleep with this on my mind?" she fires back. But he rolls over and goes to sleep. Meanwhile, she lies wide awake in bed, analyzing every word of the conversation and becoming increasingly angry as he snores loudly beside her.

Anxiety is at an all-time high in the United States. According to the National Institutes of Mental Health, more than 28 percent of American adults have an anxiety disorder, and women are 60 percent more likely to have such a disorder. Interestingly, scientists say that females—from preschool girls to elderly women—tend to worry more and have more intense worries than males. Women also have a tendency to perceive more risk in any given situation and become more anxious than men.

There are a couple reasons researchers give for why women worry more. One is that women in general have higher emotional intelligence than men. We actually feel every emotion at a higher intensity, whether that emotion is giddiness or anxiety. Reproductive hormones such as estrogen and progesterone are believed to play a role in anxiety, and these hormones are found in higher concentrations in women. Finally, according to two studies by researchers at the University of California at Davis, we are more likely to believe that past experiences forecast the future. So if we know of a similar situation in the past in which the outcome was negative, we are more likely to believe the same outcome will recur.

Following this train of thought, it is safe to say that watching the news or reruns of *Cops* can produce more anxiety in women than men. With a media culture that is increasingly filled with negative images and events, it is no wonder women are worried.

More Worries Than Women in 1972?

Let's go back to the original study I cited that claims women today are less happy than women in the early 1970s while men are continuing to see their happiness rise. If indeed it is true that women worry more, it is fair to say that today's women have a lot more to worry about. Four decades ago, a minority of women worked outside the home. Today, most women do—and that comes with a host of added responsibilities. Women feel besot by higher expectations and guilt about whether they measure up. Are you good enough? Are you doing enough? Are you attractive enough? Wealthy enough? Smart enough? Add to that the national and global worries that bombard the news—terrorism, global warming, natural disasters, and economic instability, for example. Even if you do not actively spend much time thinking about these things, they are a part of the national conversation.

Additionally, as women we are generally nurturers. We feel more responsible for others. Women in today's world have a bigger circle and community to be concerned about. We are not just in touch with family and neighbors today, but our coworkers as well. Via social media you are likely in contact with far more people than any woman was 40 years ago. And with the 24/7 news cycle, Internet news, smartphone apps, and 100 times as many channels as a woman in 1972 was exposed to, you are far more aware of so much that is going on in the world.

Just the other day, I deleted an app from a well-respected national media outlet because they kept pushing "breaking news" alerts to my phone. These breaking news alerts showed up on my phone every few hours like a text message. The problem? It was hardly ever breaking news. Often, though, it was depressing news. So I could be in the middle of having a good time when an alert sounded on my phone to tell me some bad news. I don't need that. Neither do you.

In the Midst of Chaos, Relax

You can't change the changing times, but you can change how you respond to them. No matter how much responsibility you have or how overloaded or overwhelmed you feel, relaxation can trigger positive emotions and happiness. It also has an added bonus: productivity. A 2013 *New York Times* article entitled, "Relax! You'll be More Productive," pointed out a growing body of research that shows "strategic renewal," such as short afternoon naps, more hours of sleep at night, more vacations, and more time away from the office actually increases productivity, job performance, and health. So it is essential that you learn to relax and incorporate relaxing habits into your lifestyle. Here are a few ways to do that:

1. Breathe. Deep breathing will slow your heart rate, lower your blood pressure, and leave you feeling more relaxed.

2. Trust. One of my favorite scriptures is Romans 8:28, which says, "we know that in all things God works for the good of those who love him, who have been called according to his purpose." I remember it when I begin to worry about things not going the way I'd like. Without trust, it is impossible to relax.

3. Let go of perfectionism. Few habits will do more to sabotage your ability to relax and enjoy your life than perfectionism. When you are a perfectionist, nothing is ever as it should be— and even if it is as it should be in this moment, you worry it won't stay that way. Give yourself and others permission to be human. Let go of perfectionism.

4. Don't use the news as entertainment. A better name for the news might be "the bad news." I'm not saying you shouldn't watch the news. It is important to be aware of what's going on in the world. Just don't overdose on it. Getting caught up in the punditry and gossip that has become so much of what we call news can increase your stress level and even get you worked up and agitated.

5. Get some rest. There's no getting around it: You need eight hours of sleep. Seven at a minimum. Anything less or too much more than that can negatively impact your mood as well as your mental alertness, weight, and immune system. (More about that in a moment.) Research shows that sleep acts as a daily reset button that clears out the stress of the previous day. It gives you a fresh start. But the amount of sleep we get is steadily declining. Could this be another contributor to declining female happiness? A National Sleep Foundation poll found that the average woman between the ages of 30 and 60 sleeps six hours and 41 minutes on weeknights. A 2005 NSF study showed that women are more likely to have trouble falling asleep and staying asleep and have more daytime sleepiness than men.

6. Take breaks. Your brain needs a rest. Apparently working in hour-and-a-half intervals is more productive than working straight through. So plan your breaks in 90-minute increments. You'll be more productive and experience less stress if you take a break. As you reach incremental goals in your work, you deplete your energy. It is more productive to take a break, which allows you to replenish your energy and avoid what researchers call "goal fatigue."

7. Go on vacation and do nothing. The *New York Times* article cited an internal study accounting firm Ernst & You did of its employees. They found that for each additional ten hours of vacation an employee took advantage of, their year-end performance ratings improved by eight percent. Those who vacationed frequently were also much less likely to leave the company. A change of scenery and a rest from your everyday responsibilities is an important ingredient for your happiness.

8. Take a stay-cation. When is the last time you had an opportunity to do nothing? Why not take a day or two off—or even a week!—to do just that? Talk about creating anticipation and an opportunity to relax. This simple practice is worth making a habit.

9. Meditate on the good, not the bad. Worry is meditation—meditation on all that could go wrong. Meditate instead on what might go right, what is right, and what is good.

10. Ask for help. You might be wondering how on earth you could find time to take a vacation, meditate, or relax. You're taking care of kids or trying to run a business. Good question. Your solution may lie in asking for help. Who can help give you a break? Ask for help—even if just for an hour or an afternoon. Then take some time to relax.

Are You Getting Enough Sleep to Be Happy?

Do you wake up in a bad mood? Are you one to hit the snooze button five times? According to a Duke University survey, women wake up far grumpier than their male counterparts. In fact, females need far more sleep than men and suffer more mentally and physically if forced to go without it, research suggests. According to the Centers for Disease Control, women are 50 percent more likely to report feeling tired or exhausted. Interestingly, among couples, men are more likely to disturb their mate's sleep (probably all that loud snoring, right?).

It appears lack of sleep can also put women at higher risk of heart disease, depression, and psychological problems. In contrast, men's health appears to be far less dependent on how well they sleep. In fact, men with sleeping problems showed no increased risk of the conditions that were affecting women.

If you only sleep for five or six hours during the night, try "strategic napping" during the day. But be intentional about how long you sleep. Either sleep for 25 minutes or 90 minutes. Anything in between will leave you feeling more groggy, not less.

Relaxation is largely mental. So there are a few other strategies to consider when it is time to relax. They are about your approach to life in general. Many of the women I interviewed while writing this book have a persistent feeling that they have not yet arrived. Somehow they missed the boat or there is something more they need to do or there is a decision that needs to be made. They are stuck on the "I'll be happy when" treadmill. The following strategies are about learning to "be happy while."

- Embrace what is.
- Relax in your decisions.
- Live in this season, not the next.

Embrace What Is

What would it look like to accept "what is"? We can spend so much of our energy pushing uphill against *what is*. *What is* is reality. It is the inevitable. It is the situation you wish were not in existence. You might prefer things to be a different way. You'd rather someone else was your boss. You wish your spouse's bad habit would go away. You wish your career hadn't gone off track. *What is* is the divorce you didn't want, the health challenge that burdens you, and the life that hasn't turned out quite the way you planned it.

When you resist *what is*, you live in a state of denial and anxiety. You focus your energy trying to control what is beyond your control. You spend countless days and hours focused on why it shouldn't be this way. Frustration takes over. Anger prevails. You may even hide reality to avoid facing it. Rather than letting people in on your disappointment, you keep it entirely to yourself. You may even set out to prove that *what is* really isn't. Rather than coming up with a plan to get your career back on track, you pretend everything is fine. Instead of making the most of the life you have left, you spend most of your energy lamenting the fact that things are not the way you believe they should be. Instead of accepting a loved one right where he is, you spend your energy trying to make him change. In essence, you never relax. You are always living in a state of waiting until things come together the way you want them to.

What if you stopped pushing against the inevitable and trusted your ability to handle reality? What would you do differently then? When you make that shift, it feels like releasing a heavy burden from your shoulders. It feels authentic. And let me be clear: It feels scary. At first. But if you embrace reality—finally, truly embrace where you are right now—you can relax and begin to find the courage to confront your greatest fears. You can finally move forward. You can live authentically—not in denial or fear, but in acceptance and faith and love. You cast your cares on God, trusting that all things will indeed work together for your good.

What is your "what is" right now?

_____

_____

_____

_____

What reality do you resist?

_____

_____

_____

_____

What would it look like to accept *what is*?

_____

_____

_____

_____

Relax in Your Decisions

Are you at peace? It's a simple question, but too often, in the face of a decision, we don't ask it. Sure, logic is an important element of making a decision, but so too is intuition. Rather than ignoring it or considering it secondary information, honor it. Peace is like an inner GPS system that leads you in the right direction. Even when the system looks like it's taking you on a detour, it is often offering you a shortcut, saving you the time and energy of landing in a traffic jam of confusion, bad decisions, or worse. Even in the most tumultuous situations, God can give you peace about a particular decision you need to make in the midst of the storm. You'll feel calm even though everything around you is falling to pieces. The ability to relax in the midst of a storm, to find joy despite your concerns, is found in the place of peace.

If you are honest, there have likely been times when you have felt compelled to move forward with a decision even when peace is lacking. Why is that? The reasons are probably rooted in fear—fear that if you don't make a decision now, you won't get what you want later.

This fear makes you need to be in control and that means being able to see all the pieces of the puzzle. The ones you can't see, you don't trust.

Maybe you fear that your intuition is wrong. "You don't really have the ability to hear from God himself!" your doubt says. "Don't be silly." So rather than confidently going with your gut, you forge ahead with that gnawing feeling that something's not quite right. Fear will always dampen happiness. Proverbs 22:3 promises, "The prudent see danger and take refuge, but the simple keep going and pay the penalty."

Here are a few other ways fear shows up when it's time to make a decision:

Impatience

Have you ever made a decision out of impatience? You're tired of waiting, so you move forward. Whether a simple everyday decision or a monumental one such as whom to marry or which career to choose, relax. Be patient. Choose peace while you are practicing patience. True patience isn't about *whether* you wait, it's about *how* you wait. If you believe you will only be happy when you get what you want, impatience will cause you to force things to happen out of God's timing.

Trust

Trust empowers you to relax. I'm sitting in a chair right now, totally relaxed. I trust this chair can hold me, and I trust the floor can hold this chair. I don't give it a second thought. But if I didn't trust that the chair could hold me or that the floor was not about to collapse, I could not relax while sitting here. Likewise, if you trust God, you can relax. You know he's got you. You won't utterly fall. Lack of trust in God's hand in your life shows up when you make decisions that are not rooted in peace. Trust him. If you do, impatience won't outweigh peace.

Reasoning

Some of us get very caught up in trying to figure things out. Proverbs 3:5 says, "Trust in the LORD with all your heart and lean not to your own understanding." In other words, stop trying to predict, reason, and rationalize your way into the right decisions. Overthinking is a recipe for unhappiness.

When making an important decision, going in the direction of peace is always the answer. But it takes spiritual wisdom and discernment. Relax. Get quiet. Breathe deeply. Listen. And then ask, "In this decision I am making, what choice gives me peace?"

Live in This Season, Not the Next

You and I probably both agree that wearing a wool coat in July or shorts and flip-flops in a snowstorm would be downright silly. Folks might even question the state of your mental health for that kind of behavior. But something odd seems to happen when we are impatient. Learning to relax in the current season while still preparing for the next season takes trust, patience, and wisdom. If the season you're in professionally is about learning and growing so that you can build a foundation for the future, don't miss this rich time being frustrated that the future isn't here yet. If you do, you'll miss the abundant lessons being offered and you may even miss the opportunities that will unfold after you learn those lessons. Missing this season could mean you're totally unprepared when the next season comes.

Know your season. Dress for it. Embrace it. It can save you a great deal of anxiety and allow you to relax rather than spend your time frustrated. Why do we often insist on being in a season other than the one we are in, pushing to get out of it and get on with the next thing? It is often because we don't trust the process. We think God must not be clued in to our lives and we need to help him along. We don't understand that progress is a process—and it's not always a quick, convenient process. But when you really trust that God has you in the palm of his hand, you can relax even in the stormiest of seasons. It's temporary. Seasons always are. Some are longer than others, but eventually seasons change.

In what way are you dressed for a season other than the one you're in? In what way are you insisting things be different in order for you to be happy? In what way are you showing up in a wool coat in the heat of summer? It might not be the season for you to spend much. This season may be about saving and self-control. This may not be the season for a relationship. Perhaps God is calling you to heal and be still in his presence before you jump into another romance. I don't know what this means for your life, but you do. Be happy in this season. Each one has a purpose. Each one is to be celebrated for its own reasons. Refuse to judge your season. Simply be determined to glean the lesson from it—and be happy in it.

What season are you in?

_____

_____

_____

_____

In what way are you operating out of season, being impatient, or resisting the inevitable?

_____

_____

_____

_____

What would it look like to relax and be happy while you wait for that season you long for?

_____

_____

_____

_____

Activate This Happiness Trigger!

- Take breaks every 90 minutes.
- Breathe deeply.
- Turn off the news, loud noise, and anything else not soothing.
- Schedule a stay-cation to stay home and do absolutely nothing!
- Stop worrying about decisions and allow peace to guide you.
- Rather than fighting the inevitable, embrace what is.
- Choose to be happy while you wait for the next season of your life rather than waiting to be happy when the next season comes.

CONVERSATION STARTER:

Relax. There's Nothing to Fix!

*Why you should stop trying to fix your
life and start embracing it "as is"*

Points to ponder:

- Trusting God doesn't mean trusting him to do what you asked him to do. It means trusting him no matter what he chooses to do.

- Until you learn to be happy without what you thought you had to have, you will not be happy when you get it. The hedonic treadmill ensures you'll find something else you insist you need in order to be happy.

Conversation Starters

- What have you been trying to fix in your life?

- In what way(s) have you felt like you "missed the boat" and must make up for lost time?

- What would it feel like for you to surrender your desires to God's will?

Praying out loud when I'm alone hasn't traditionally been my habit. But one morning, a few months before I turned 40, it hit me: What am I being quiet for? Nobody's here but me and God. On that day I was running late, so I decided to pray out loud while I made up the bed.

As I pondered a litany of anxiety-producing topics, my prayer went something like this:

"Lord, I want to be married again. Lord, you know I want children, and well, *I'm about to turn 40*. I'm running out of time, God.

And just in case maybe I didn't pray the previous prayers right, I'm just praying right now for the desires of my heart. I mean, your Word says if I delight myself in you, you'll give me those desires. And, I mean, I believe you. But I'm just saying, *could you speed it up and fix this situation?*"

That's when I heard a simple, profound statement in my spirit. I believe it was God's message to me. This is what I heard:

"There's nothing to fix."

I stopped in my tracks at the foot of the bed. Peace enveloped me as I felt a burden lift. The shift was immediate. I pondered it several more times. *There's nothing to fix.*

There is something truly liberating about contentment. About being okay with exactly where you are in life right now. I'm not talking about having no desires or ambition for something more. I'm talking about simultaneously feeling at peace with not striving. It is comforting to embrace the concept that "there's nothing to fix."

One of the reason I believe women are less happy than decades ago is that we are bombarded with expectations about what our lives are supposed to look like. If you're single, you can feel you need to fix that problem and get married. If you're married, you can be miserable and feel you need to fix your spouse or the marriage itself. If you have kids, you need to fix your parenting skills or fix your kids. If you don't have kids, you need to fix that too. If you have a career, you need to fix the fact that you are not further ahead in it. If you are a stay-at-home parent, you may feel inadequate for not doing something more outside the home. Whatever season of life you are in, if you take in the constant barrage of expectations, you can spend all your time feeling that you need to fix something. It is exhausting. It is never-ending. And it saps your happiness.

What have you been feeling the pressure to "fix"? What would it look like to surrender? For the first time that day at the foot of my bed, I surrendered. I gave it up. I detached myself from the outcome and decided that my happiness would not and could not be dependent upon "fixing" my life. For the first time, I felt like everything would be okay. I decided I would trust God no matter what happened. And when I finally did that, something beautiful happened.

My focus shifted from fixing my life to creating my life. I began to dream of all that my life could be—just as it was. In other words, if the circumstances I had no control over never changed, what would I create in my life? Without the burden of holding my breath and hoping for the right husband and some children, I said, "Valorie, what do you want to do with the life you have right now?"

I want to go to Italy. I want to visit every continent. I want to enjoy my family more. I want to have my goddaughter and little cousins visit their Auntie Val on spring break and during the summer. I want to be more generous and find people to help. I want to pay off my mortgage. I want to indulge my journalistic side and start interviewing people. I want to host a television show. I want to volunteer doing work that is fulfilling for me and helpful for the people who need it. Just writing this list fills me with joy and happiness.

When I let go of what I believed my life "should" be, I was free to focus on making my life what it could be *right now*. All the things I just mentioned are things I had the ability to begin actively moving toward. And I've got a feeling that while I am fruitfully living with that kind of passion and joy, I will stumble upon a life that is more than I could ever ask, think, or imagine.

How about you? In what way(s) is it time to stop trying to fix things and just relax?

Winning Words

*Why it's hard for pessimists to be happy and how
anyone can learn to be more optimistic*

Decision:

"Every day I speak words of hope, peace, and love."

You've heard it many times: You are what you think. But thoughts often become words before they become actions. So it's safe to say this: You are also what you say. In fact, neuroscientists have now proven that just saying powerful words can make you more powerful. For example, when you lift a weight, saying a word such as *strong* increases the force with which you lift that weight. Amazing, isn't it? Proverbs 18:21 says, "The tongue has the power of life and death." This is literally true, scientifically proven: Life and death *is* in the power of the tongue.

I tested it out just yesterday while doing a crazy workout video in which the guy leading the exercises kept looking into the camera and telling me to "dig deeper." Panting, sweating, and out of breath, I wanted to tell him to shut up. But he kept saying it, kept encouraging me…and so I kept digging deeper for more energy and strength. And you know what? It worked. Whether it is a word of encouragement from someone else or the words you speak to encourage yourself, words are powerful.

In fact, positive language is a happiness trigger. "Winning words" trigger positive emotions and chemicals in the brain that cause you to feel happier and stronger. There are several ways to use your words to boost your happiness. I list them here and then we'll discuss each one a bit more:

1. Speak in the affirmative.
2. Surround yourself with positive words.
3. Shorten your sob story.
4. Write about your best possible future self—in the present tense.
5. Receive positive words.
6. Use words to bounce back.

> From the fruit of their lips people are filled with good things (Proverbs 12:14).

Speak in the Affirmative

Say these statements aloud, slowly and intentionally.

- I can do it.
- My dream is possible.
- I am happy about _____.
- God loves me.
- I am loved and loveable.
- I am blessed.
- I am grateful for _____.
- I have gifts and talents that make the world a better place.
- I like who I am becoming.

What emotions do you feel after stating those words? Are the emotions positive? It may seem a little hokey to make positive statements out loud, but after making such statements most women feel lighter, stronger, happier, and more optimistic.

Researchers in France concluded that using positive sentence structures sends messages to the brain that produce positive results.[1] For example, if you say, "Yes, I can do it!" while trying to grip an object, you grip it with greater force. But if you say, "I will not fail at this," you do not get the same effect. The key to speaking in the affirmative is to structure your sentences in terms of the outcome you want rather than the outcome you do not want. So rather than, "I don't want to be sad," you say, "I want to be happy." Rather than talking in terms of what you are against, talk about what you are *for*. It is an intentional focus on the positive—what you want more of in your life and relationships. This change in how you use your words is simple, but it inspires a different energy than a focus on the negative.

When you state things in the negative, you think about the negative. What do you think of when you see the statement "I'm tired of fighting with my kids"? You likely envision exactly the words the statement evokes—someone fighting with their kids. But what do you think of when you hear "I want a home environment that is peaceful"? Most likely, you picture a peaceful environment. Use your words to evoke positive images of what you want to manifest. Speak in the affirmative.

Surround Yourself with Positive Words

What words do you see daily in your environment? On your computer screen? In the art on your walls? The vision board you keep in your office? If you use words in your environment, make sure they are uplifting ones.

Studies have also shown the release of happy hormones in the brain when we look at a positive word, such as *yes* or *love*, and the release of stress-inducing hormones when we look at negative words, such as *no* or *hate*. Words matter. Words have the power to shift your mood—immediately. Take a look at the words on this list. First look at the negative ones, then the positive ones. Notice the difference in how you feel.

Yes!	No!
Love	Hate
Abundance	Poverty
Blessings	War

Beautiful	Fight
Strong	Disgust
Happy	Stupid
Excited	Depressed
Cheerful	Ugly
Laughter	Evil

What positive words would you like to see every day? What do you want to be reminded of?

Shorten Your Sob Story

One way you can sabotage your happiness is by over-talking the negative events of your life. When first dealing with a difficult season, it is normal and even necessary to talk about it so you can process it. But eventually, it is time to move on. When you go into lengthy descriptions of negative events, you can get drawn back into the emotion of it. You've probably had it happen before, haven't you? You are having a perfectly good day and someone brings up that old situation that always gets you worked up! Don't take the bait. Once you've worked through a particular problem or issue, don't rehash it. Shorten your sob story to 30 to 60 seconds.

Write About Your Best Possible Future Self— In the Present Tense

In *Successful Women Think Differently*, I shared an exercise called "Your Best Possible Future Self." Researcher Dr. Laura King discovered there are health benefits when we write about realizing our own potential in the present tense. Those who do so have been shown to have stronger immune systems, making them less susceptible to colds. Depending on your vision of your best possible future self, you might write something like this:

I am healthy and happy. I move my body daily and eat plenty of fruits and vegetables. In fact, I love eating healthy, home-cooked meals! My husband is my best friend and my marriage is strong. We are wonderful examples for our children of what it means to be in a healthy relationship. At work, I am excellent but not stressed by what I do. I enjoy my coworkers and I am respected for my contributions. Financially, we are debt-free, have an emergency fund, and are actively saving to retire at age 50. We are getting ready for a vacation to the beach in the next two months and I am so excited to be able to take time to relax regularly!

Do you get the picture? Try it. Write words in the present tense about who you are one year from now.

Receive Positive Words

Thoughts often become words before they become actions. But it also happens in reverse. Words become thoughts and then actions follow those thoughts. This is particularly true of the words of others. You cannot control what comes out of someone else's mouth—whether a friend or family member or a character on television. That's why it is crucial to be intentional about who and what you allow into your environment. If the people you spend the most time with are pessimistic, eventually you may notice yourself becoming more pessimistic. If most of what you watch on television is doom and gloom, don't be surprised if you feel emotionally drained when you get up off of the sofa. If your music is a chorus of bitter love songs, no wonder you've given up hope. Protect your mind by limiting the negative words you are exposed to.

I often joke that my writing talent was born of the words of my second grade teacher, Ms. Johnson. She told me I was a good writer. And I believed her! After all, she was an expert, right? She should have known. I wrote poetry—short little diddies like this one:

I like to walk and talk and play with chalk
Rip and run and play in the sun.

That's it. Short and sweet. From that, she deduced I had talent. She sent my poems off to kids' magazines and even got one of them published. For the rest of my school days, I behaved as though I had talent. When it came to writing, I had confidence. I could always hear her saying assuredly, "You are a good writer."

In order to benefit from the positive words of others, you must be willing to receive them. From now on, refuse to reject others' positive words when spoken into your life. Even if it is uncomfortable, simply say *thank you*. Receive it. But when negative, untrue words are spoken, reject them. Recognize that others' opinions are just that—opinions, not fact. Don't be afraid to use your words to speak up for yourself and set boundaries when necessary. Receive the positive and reject the negative. When it comes to receiving positive words, make sure to set boundaries with others, be careful what you watch, be intentional about what you listen to, and be selective about what you read.

Use Words to Bounce Back

The most powerful words are the ones you speak to yourself. It has been said that we believe what we say more than we believe what others say. What are you saying to yourself about yourself, about your potential, about your life?

When I speak on resilience, I often teach a very simple formula adapted from the work of Dr. Aaron Beck, considered the father of cognitive behavioral therapy. This approach acknowledges that our destiny and psychological well-being is not simply a manifestation of what happened in our childhoods and we can't fix it simply by looking back and trying to figure out why we do what we do. Instead, behavior is changed by changing what you think—that is, what you say in your own mind. We tend to believe that how we feel and behave is a result of what happens to us—our circumstances. But the truth is that how you feel is determined by what you say to yourself about your circumstances. Your words are powerful, especially the ones in your mind.

So remember this little formula. I call it TTR—Trigger, Thoughts, and Reactions. A trigger is any event, conversation, stressor, or adversity your face. Your thoughts are what you say to yourself about the trigger. Your reactions are your feelings or your actions as a result. The key to your happiness (how you feel about your life and what you do every day) lies not in the triggers you face, but in your thoughts about those triggers. Change what you say to yourself and you change how you feel. Happy women say different things about their circumstances than unhappy women. This is why you can have two women going through similar circumstances and have a totally different outlook on life.

It is within your control to boost your happiness by changing what you say to yourself. When faced with difficult circumstances, these are the kinds of words unhappy women say to themselves:

- Bad things always happen to me.
- I'm so unlucky.
- My life is over. My best days are behind me.
- I can't.
- I'm not good/smart/attractive/rich enough.
- There's no hope.
- I can't do anything right.
- I'm afraid, therefore I can't do it. I'm stuck.
- I give up.

In the face of the same circumstances, happy women use *winning words* to climb out of a difficult circumstance:

- I got a bad break, but that's life and I'm not giving up.

- I failed, but I'm learning from it and eventually I will succeed.
- I have enough of whatever I need to do the things I am called to do.
- I've been disappointed, but I will not give up hope!
- I made a mistake. I am correcting it.
- The best is yet to come.

Choose your words intentionally. Choose words that give you hope, inspire you, and lift you. It is your choice.

Activate This Happiness Trigger!

- Strategically place positive words and inspiring quotes in your environment that make you feel hopeful—on your desk, in your home, or on your computer screen.
- Rather than talking about what you don't want, structure your sentences to state what you do want.
- Take a few minutes to describe your best possible future self in the present tense.
- Refuse to be pulled into negative conversations and dredge up old wounds and negative emotions unnecessarily. Shorten your sob story.
- Get together with your friend who is an encourager.
- Speak words of encouragement to others. It is a powerful way to serve.

Winning Words or Whining Words?

Choosing to see your glass as half full

Points to Ponder

- Optimists are more likely to succeed at reaching goals, effectively leading others, and being happy, especially in the face of setbacks.

- Choose to see the glass as half full, but acknowledge your disappointments. Be authentic, but kindle your hope.

- Realistic optimism balances the truth with hope and vision for the future.

Conversation Starters

- Have you ever pretended everything was okay when inside you felt completely the opposite? When? Why? What was the result? What would you do differently if given the chance?

- When it comes to a tough scenario you are not happy about, are you using winning words or whining words?

As I interviewed women around the country, a woman's attitude toward her relationships—and her relationship status (married, unmarried)—seemed to be one of the biggest contributing factors to her happiness or lack thereof. Initially, I thought it was the woman's relationships that made the difference. For example, many women I talked to were single—some divorced, some never married. Almost all of the women who were single wanted to be married. Most, but not all, of the women who did not have children wanted them. And while some were clearly depressed about the lack of a husband or child and even pessimistic about the prospect of one, others embraced their current season of life and maintained hope for love and family in the future. Consider this comment from Allie on Facebook, who admittedly would welcome marriage and children:

> I'll be 40 in a month. I have no kids, I've never been married, and I have a great life. Surround yourself with good people and get rid of the riffraff! I'm one heck of an aunt—that's for sure!

Contrast this with a message from another woman named Melissa, newly divorced with a beautiful child:

> I've been crying every day. I'll be 40 soon and life isn't what I thought it would be. I feel very insignificant.

And then there's this comment from Angela:

> I've been married 12 years and I can't say it's a happy marriage. But I'm trying to make the most of it. Divorce is not an option for either of us.

These three women are all in very different relationship circumstances, with varying attitudes about where they stand in life. Some would say Allie is kidding herself—that she's not being honest. Can she really be satisfied with being an aunt and never a mom, if that's what she wants? Women like Allie would say, "But I don't have kids. I don't have a husband at this time. So what's the point of me ruminating about that? How is it going to help me? Why not make the most of where I am while hoping for something more?" Clearly, her attitude about marriage contributes to her happiness. This is a prime example of the power of your thoughts, which is the key to resilience.

What Are You Saying to Yourself About Your Circumstances?

Ultimately, your attitude about your relationship status is derived from your innermost thoughts. What are you saying to yourself about your circumstances? And is what you're saying helping you or hurting you? These two questions are simple, but profound. Consider Allie, for example. She is saying to herself, "My life is great. It can be great without a husband and children. And if I get married and have children, that can be great too. I choose not to put marriage on a pedestal as a cure-all for unhappiness."

Melissa, on the other hand, has said some things that are quite the opposite: "I am very insignificant. Life hasn't turned out as planned and therefore, I am miserable. Forty is looming and I've failed if life doesn't look a specific way at that age." Her thoughts are clearly hurting her. This is not to say she doesn't have something to mourn. The death of a marriage is extremely painful. I would never minimize that. However, when you experience something so disappointing and devastating, it is even more critical to pay attention to what you say to yourself about that circumstance. You can prolong your recovery by overstating the devastation. When you give meaning to your circumstances that weakens you emotionally and mentally, you sabotage your own recovery and eventual happiness. The key is to align your thoughts with God's loving thoughts of you and your circumstances.

Let's take a look at Angela's thoughts again. She has resigned herself to an unhappy marriage. She isn't seeking counseling. But she is committed, and that's a big positive. Unless she is committed to being miserable, though, she needs to ask a few questions. What incremental goals could she and her husband set? What steps could they take to improve the marriage? What do they want the marriage to be a year from now or a decade from now? By beginning to paint a vision for the future, it will become clearer which direction they should move in next.

Positive attitude or positive spin? How do you determine the difference? A positive attitude is about believing in the possibilities for the future. Positive spin is putting a happy mask on an unhappy situation. It is not authentic. It might not even be true. Tapping into your faith and using winning words to trigger happiness only works if you're being authentic.

Movement

*Why exercise can be as effective as antidepressants
and how to make it a lifestyle*

Decision:

"I spend 30 minutes each day moving my body."

I just came back in from a "wog"—that's what I call the power walking I do with a little intermittent jogging. I know for sure I feel more alive and energetic than I did when I left. My head is clear and even though I am sitting now, and not walking, I am still breathing more deeply. My lungs feel expanded, like I could belt out a Whitney Houston ballad. (I am aware it would not sound like Whitney, but I still feel like I could do it!) I don't wog to lose weight. The main reason I do it is because it makes me feel good. My secondary reason is to be healthy, but "being healthy" is not a result I see immediately after I take a power walk. Feeling good is.

Let me be clear. Today, I headed out of the house with ease. However, there are days when I put on my exercise clothes with the intention of working out and end up wearing my workout clothes until it's time to go to bed. Have you ever had one of those days? You meant to get to it, but distractions seemed more enticing, you never got focused, and your plan was upended. It happens to most of us from time to time. Exercise, though, seems easier to put off than other goals. One of the reasons might be that the results we perceive exercise will give us are not immediate. In other words, we think of it the wrong way. Rather than focusing on the delayed gratification of a longer life, healthier

heart, and a desirable dress size, perhaps we need to focus on the immediate benefit exercise provides: a boost in happiness.

Maybe you've connected the dots between movement and happiness. Maybe you haven't. If not, right now is a perfect time to shift
your perspective.

Happiness Is a Better Motivator Than Delayed Gratification

Movement is a happiness trigger. Whether it's your spin class or a
walk in the park or salsa dancing or some jumping jacks, moving your
body literally boosts your well-being. I don't call this happiness trigger
"exercise" because I simply don't think of it that way. Besides, too many
women (maybe you are one of them) don't have positive associations
with exercise. Too many only think of exercise as something to do for
the delayed gratification of losing weight or preventing heart disease or
lowering your cholesterol. On the list of 24 character strengths in the
Values in Action (VIA) classifications of strengths, particularly among
those in the Western world, "discipline and self-control" lands near the
bottom. Discipline is hardly a motivator for most of us. Happiness, on
the other hand, is a motivator. Happiness is the one thing that we pursue for its own sake. Everything else in life, we generally pursue because
we believe it will make us happy—whether it's a relationship or career
endeavor or that new house or even a relationship with God. I'm far
happier and at peace with God in my life than without him.

So what if you pursued movement because it would make you happier? Not because you'll lose some weight. Not because the doctor said
it is what you have to do. But because when you get moving, your
blood circulation and oxygen flow increases, endorphins are released,
your mind clears, and *you feel happier*. Happy women get moving. And
because they move their bodies, they feel better—*right away*. You want
to lift your mood right now? Start moving! In fact, if you take a few
minutes in this moment to get moving, I promise you'll experience an
upward shift in your mood. According to Gallup research, participants
who engaged in exercise for just 20 minutes could still feel a significant boost in their mood even 12 hours later compared with those who
engaged in no physical activity.[1] I don't know about you, but most of

us waste 20 minutes easily in a day. What if you spent that time moving your body to boost your mood?

Multiple studies dating back more than three decades confirm that regular exercise can be as effective as antidepressants for patients dealing with mild to moderate depression. Those who were consistent in their exercise regimen were less likely to relapse. A 1999 study published in the *Archives of Internal Medicine* divided participants suffering depression into three groups. One group participated in an aerobic program, another was prescribed and took the antidepressant Zoloft, and a third group did both. After four months, more than 60 percent of the participants could no longer be classified as depressed.[2]

Even if you are not dealing with depression, though, exercise is a happiness booster. If you're already happy, it'll make you feel even better. If you are neutral, it can bring on the happy feelings by increasing circulation and oxygen flow and releasing feel-good chemicals into your body.

Doing Nothing Makes You Tired

It may seem counterintuitive, but inactivity is a recipe for exhaustion. We were made to move. And when we don't, immobility drains our energy. Any exercise is better than no exercise. Do *something*. Keep some light weights near your desk or by the sofa and do lifts while you take a break or watch your favorite television show. Often a lack of energy has more to do with being inactive than it does with age. When you feel tired or blue, that's actually the most important time to exercise. It energizes you—literally. Every day. If you want to be consistently happy and healthy, exercise should not be an option, but a non-negotiable part of your life. The real question is, how could you make it so? What would you be willing to do consistently that qualifies as legitimate exercise? It may sound like a funny question, but I'm dead serious. You've got to find something. Otherwise exercise becomes a struggle, a back-and-forth tug of war. Two months on, two months off. That's not what you want or need.

No Excuses! 8 Ways to Get Moving Now

1. Do jumping jacks. Exercise pioneer Jack LaLanne had the right idea: Jumping in place and flapping your arms is a good way to get moving—right now. No equipment required. Pretend like you're in your first grade PE class. You can do jumping jacks by the bed, in front of the sofa, in the backyard, or wherever the mood strikes.

2. Take stretch breaks. One of the best ways to boost your energy when you've been sedentary for a long time is by stretching. It is great to do when you wake up, after sitting and working for a long time, or during a break on a long car ride.

3. Play hide-and-seek or video games that promote exercise with your kids. Kids will get you moving! Play with them. Not only will it help you get moving, but it will help them get moving too. With childhood obesity and diabetes on the rise, there are few better gifts to give your kids than getting them in the habit of moving.

4. Join a sports league or start your own—tennis, golf, softball, basketball, or anything you choose! Guys are great at this. It is one of the ways they bond—by playing games. As women, we need to take note. Playing sports is a great way to connect with others, get your body moving, and have fun all at once.

5. Take a dance class. This isn't just for couples, although taking up a dance class with your honey is one fun way to get moving and enjoy quality time together. But you don't need a partner to take a class. Ask around in your city. You should be able to find adult classes for hip-hop, jazz, tap, or swing dancing. Whether at the gym, community college, or a dance studio, sign up and start dancing! I took a tap dancing class as an adult. It was creative and lots of fun.

6. Exercise ten minutes at a time, three times a day. Feel like you don't have time to get moving? Break it up. There is no rule that your 30 minutes of exercise have to occur in one lump. Ten

minutes in the morning, afternoon, and evening—whenever you can squeeze it in—is just as effective.

7. Go for a brisk walk. Many doctors say walking is even better than running because it is easier on your body, especially your joints. It is easy. Find the time and do it. Here's a little inspiration for you: My mother, who uses a walker due to her disabilities, walks two and half miles four days a week. If she can do it, you can do it!

8. Turn on your favorite music and dance in your living room. My first memory of dancing was in the living room. I was dancing with my mom and a childhood friend, Tyrone, to Michael Jackson's *Off the Wall* album. I was about five years old and I wanted to know how to do "the rock," so my mom showed us. It was a dance Michael did to his song "Rock with You" on his first solo album in the late 1970s. Every time I think of that memory, I smile. So it should come as no surprise that I still dance in my living room! I love to dance. It is great exercise. I'll turn on my favorite gospel artist, rock artist, pop artist—just depends on my mood—and get moving! Try it. It is a fun, easy way to get your heart pumping. No class to drive to. No videos to buy. Just pure fun.

Fuel to Get You Moving

To get moving more easily, you need the right fuel. There are foods that boost your mood and there are foods that can ruin it.

My client Shirley was frustrated by how tired she seemed to be every afternoon. Typically, her energy plummeted between two and three o'clock. With back-to-back meetings, she thought it was simply the exhaustion of having to be "on" all day. When she took a two-week vacation, she expected to get her energy back. With plenty of sleep at night and no meetings or projects looming, she was perplexed when—around 2:30 every afternoon—she found herself feeling groggy and tired.

With no explanation, she decided to go to the doctor. The doctor asked a lot of questions, but one of them was about her diet.

Although Shirley is a healthy weight, her size is more attribut-able to good genes and a high metabolism than a good diet. Most days, she has coffee and two donuts for breakfast and opts for fast food at lunch and dinner. She knows it isn't good for her, but it's quick and she loves the taste, she says. "I almost feel addicted," she said. "I have my favorite three or four fast food restaurant meals and I just rotate to different spots on different days of the week. It's cheap and fast, and that fits my needs because I am quite busy." As it turns out, Shirley's diet contributed to her exhaustion as well as the feelings of sadness she sometimes experienced but didn't talk much about. A regular diet of pizza, hamburgers, hotdogs, and processed snacks is linked to depression and lethargy. So be intentional about fueling your body with the kinds of foods that will actually make you feel good.

Eat Yourself Happy: Foods That Boost Your Mood

- Bananas: The sugar and fiber make them a super energy food. Add peanut butter for protein and a banana makes a healthy snack.

- Brown rice: It is high in manganese, which is a mineral that produces energy from carbohydrates and protein.

- Almonds: These nuts make a terrific snack to keep in a bag in your purse or at your desk because they are packed with protein, manganese, and riboflavin.

- Salmon: It contains protein, vitamin B6, niacin, and ribo-flavin, which help convert all the food you eat into energy.

- Asparagus: It's full of tryptophan, which helps process serotonin, also known as the "happy hormone."

- Sweet potatoes: This superfood is high in vitamin A and vitamin C and can ward off mid-day fatigue. Try mashed sweet potatoes or sauté or bake them in strips to make sweet potato fries.

- Honey: It is a natural sweetener that boosts energy. Use in herbal tea for an afternoon kick.

- Spinach: This is a terrific source of iron, which helps your body produce more energy. It also contains phenyl-ethylamine, which helps ward off chemicals that lead to depression. It makes a great choice for a salad, or sauté a little spinach as a side dish or mix it in with your eggs for breakfast.

- Grass-fed meat: Animals that are raised on grass have more linoleum acid, a "happy fat" that slows stress hormones and protects brain cells.

- Avocados: They contain a lot of vitamin B3, a serotonin-boosting ingredient, as well as omega-3 fatty acids, which have been linked to a healthy brain and boosted mood.

- Eggs: Eggs are full of L-tryptophan, which helps boost the hormones that make you feel happy.

- Apples: Apples are high in fiber and because they take longer to digest, the energy boost you get will last longer.

Activate This Happiness Trigger!

- Stop right now and do 20 jumping jacks or stretch for two minutes.

- Turn on a song that energizes you and dance for the full length of the song.

- Instead of a snack from the vending machine, fuel your body with an apple or banana and a handful of nuts.

- Incorporate 30 minutes of exercise into your lifestyle four days a week.

- Make moving a social endeavor. Sign up for a dance class, take lessons in swimming, tennis, or golf, or join the women's softball league in your community.

Do You Like How You Look?

Points to Ponder

- Research indicates that women of all ages are happier when they feel attractive.
- Men are called "distinguished" when they get gray hair and wrinkles. Women are told to cover the gray and use anti-aging products.
- Nobody on a magazine cover really looks like that. You do know that, right? Those photos have been airbrushed until they hardly resemble the original picture.
- Body image issues impact women at much higher rates than men.

Conversation Starters

- Are you happy with your looks? If not, what do you want to change and why?
- Why do some women tend to compete with each other in the looks department?
- How do you embrace a new standard of beauty when your youth begins to fade?

For years, I did not like my hair. I did everything I could to straighten it, lengthen it, or weave it. My decision to go natural in 2008 was the result of a conversation I'd had with a British male friend years earlier. He'd asked if I could do my hair like the singer Macy Gray. She was new on the scene at the time and when I went to her website and saw the natural 'fro she was rocking, I laughed hysterically at the fact that he thought my hair would do *that*.

"No," I explained. "My hair is relaxed."

Not having a clue what that meant, he probed further. "Relaxed?" he said curiously. "Is your hair uptight?"

I almost fell out of my chair. "You could say that," I responded as I chuckled at his question. "I use chemicals to straighten it."

He was intrigued. "So is that what all black women do or is that just something you do?"

"Most black women with straight hair did something to straighten it," I explained. Then he asked a question that stuck with me for years.

"Why don't you just wear it the way it grows out of your head?"

That one straightforward question led me on an inner journey to discover what my natural hair was like. It had been relaxed since I was six years old. When you live next to the beach, the humidity is a bear.

When I finally started wearing it the way it grew out of my head, it felt good. It made me happier when I looked in the mirror. For the first time as an adult, I actually loved my hair. Whether it is our hair or thighs or nose or size, it seems women are much harder on themselves about their looks than men. But then, so is our culture. Women in television news have careers that often don't last past the age of 50, while men do. Female actresses see fewer leading roles as they get older—men see more. Women in positions of power are routinely judged by their hair, weight, and wardrobe choices. This is rarely the case for men. Research says that as men get older, their happiness continues an upward trend, but as women get older they become sadder. I can't help but wonder if a part of that equation is the pressure to look perfect. What do you think?

Savoring

When you learn to revel in the moment,
you learn to truly live.

Decision:

"Every day, I enjoy a moment worth savoring."

This past spring, my goddaughter wanted to come spend a few days with me during her spring break. One of the reasons I moved to Atlanta was so I could be close in proximity to the people I love most—my family. So the fact that Destiny asked to come stay with her godmother/cousin/namesake (we share our middle name) tickled me to no end. The first evening, after arriving home and eating dinner, she wanted to watch the Disney Channel. Perfect. Let me tell you, sometimes I watch the Disney Channel to de-stress—even when there are no kids anywhere near me. It may sound silly, but honestly, there's not much worth watching on television these days and sometimes the news pundits and gossip are just plain stressful.

Destiny and I laid on opposite ends of the sofa and watched *Dog with a Blog*. Soon, I was having trouble keeping my eyes open. So Destiny attempted to wake me up with the exciting news that the movie *A Bug's Life* was up next. She came to my end of the sofa and snuggled up next to me to watch it together. Neither of us made it through the movie. When I woke up just after midnight, Destiny was sound asleep, her head tucked just under my arm peacefully as she slept quietly. I smiled, grateful for my time with her. Soon, she won't want to watch animated movies on the sofa with her 40-something godmother. But for now, she does. What a blessing.

Savoring special moments as they happen is an important happiness skill. And in our hectic, nonstop world, it is easy to miss moments like this. If you want to be happy though, you can't miss these moments. They are moments of peace and joy and connection. Sometimes we miss out on what life is really about because we are never actually living in the present. We are thinking about the next moment or the next week. And if not the future, we think about what happened in the past. It is one thing to intentionally savor the past and anticipate the future as a way to appreciate what's happened and build excitement about what's to come. It is something entirely different to miss the present moment because you never take time to savor it.

How Do You "Savor"?

If you are perpetually busy, feeling like you race through life and do everything by the seat of your pants, savoring will take some practice. We live in a culture that is so fast-paced and so focused on packing in as many experiences as possible that it can be easy to not actually experience any of them. Savoring begins with slowing down. I have found the best way to do that is by breathing.

Even in this moment, as you read these words, is your breath shallow? If so, take a deep breath. Notice the feeling of air entering your nostrils. Can you feel the slight sensation of your breath against your skin? Feel the air as it enters your lungs, expanding and stretching your rib cage. Now, take your breath to a deeper place. On your next breath, rather than expanding your rib cage, breathe deeply into your belly. Feel your abdomen expand as you inhale. Then upon exhaling, open your mouth and hear your voice as the air whispers, "Ahhhh." You ought to feel the oxygen as it flushes your brain. Your blood pressure may even have lowered a little. And you feel more relaxed and calm. You just savored your breath—the most basic gift of God. Each time you breathe consciously, remind yourself that when you feel your breath, you feel life itself.

Savoring is to live consciously attuned to the blessing of this current moment in time. For most of us, it takes practice. My mind seems to so easily venture to the future that savoring is almost always an intentional choice. I am reminded of the scripture in Matthew 6:34: "Do not worry about tomorrow, for tomorrow will worry about itself." Be present today. Here are some very practical ways to savor:

1. Breathe slowly and deeply. In addition to being an act of savoring itself, breathing slows down your thinking, lowers your stress, and brings you into the present moment.

2. Place your feet on the ground. If you're little like me, this might mean scooting up to the front of the chair because otherwise your legs are typically dangling. But if you are the average height for a woman or tall, this is easy. Feel your feet on the floor. It grounds you and makes you aware of your body.

3. Eat slowly. I love good food, don't you? Most of the time, though, we eat too quickly. We do other things while eating—talk on the phone, check text messages, or catch up on reading. None of these are negatives in and of themselves, but multitasking while eating typically means you don't fully enjoy it. Make eating an experience. Use your good dishes. Don't swallow as soon as you take a bite. Instead, savor your bite for a moment. Taste the flavors. Then swallow. Not only is this a more conscious way to eat, but it typically means you'll eat less and digest your food more easily. By the time most people get the signal from the stomach to the brain that they are full, they are well past the point at which they should have stopped eating!

4. Set boundaries around your conversations. Have you ever talked to someone who responds to every outside distraction while talking with you? You're mid-sentence on the phone when they start talking to someone who is walking by. You're having dinner and they keep responding to text messages and phone calls. It is annoying and it sends a message that everything else is more important to them in that moment. Engage in conscious conversation. This may mean shorter conversations sometimes

as you juggle multiple responsibilities, but the conversations will be of a higher quality.

5. Set boundaries around your activities. Likewise, protect precious moments and important activities by setting boundaries that minimize interruptions. Remember that interruptions decrease happiness, according to research. It is difficult to savor a moment when you are being continually disturbed by something unrelated.

6. Feel the emotion of the moment. Something else that gets lost when you don't savor your moments is the feeling of the moment. When I noticed the simplicity of the moment on the sofa with my goddaughter, I felt several emotions: joy, peace, gratitude, and love. Because I allowed myself to feel those emotions in the moment as I savored it, I can now reminisce and write about the experience because I remember it quite well. I was there! I was fully present in that moment. Therefore it was rich and meaningful even though it was also small and simple. Without intentionally "feeling the emotion," you can have big, long-anticipated experiences and not remember much about them. Why? Because you were not really there. You were present physically, but not emotionally, mentally, or spiritually.

Savor the Everyday Moments

To trigger your happiness every day, you must be conscious of the everyday treats that surround you. For example, I just came in from sitting on my patio. It is a sunny, warm day and I thought it would be good to get some sun. So rather than staying in the house to read my daily *Jesus Calling* devotional and the Anna Quindlen memoir I've been enjoying, I decided to sit outside and read. After 15 minutes, sunny and warm started to feel like hot and sweaty, so now I'm sitting at my dining room table. The door to the patio is open, so I can hear the birds chirping and it sounds so melodic. I'm writing to you, and that brings me joy. I'm savoring this moment. And while you are reading this in a future moment that hasn't taken place as I type these words, my hope is that you are savoring this moment as you read them.

It is the everyday moments that are most important to savor because they are the most common. If you hold your breath to savor only the off-the-charts amazing moments that happen in life, you'll spend most of your life waiting on those moments to arrive. If instead you open your eyes to the miracle and gift of each moment, happiness is bound to follow you all the days of your life.

So yes, savor the big moments. But even more important, savor the little ones because those come every day. In fact, they come every minute, every hour, of every day. As an exercise, I challenge you to make a list of everyday moments you normally rush through or experience on autopilot. These are moments that you can make an intentional choice to start savoring, beginning today. Close your eyes for a moment and think about the multiple everyday moments you normally experience that you'd like to get more joy out of. I'll start the list with a few ideas and you finish it:

1. Eating a meal. Savor the opportunity to taste the flavors of your food and give your body the nourishment it needs. You may just find that consciously savoring your food inspires you to eat healthier foods that are more enjoyable to savor.

2. Commuting to and from work. I know. If you have a stressful commute, this one may sound ridiculous, but really it isn't. The more stressful your commute, the more important it is to find a way to savor it. Find a new way to think of the commute. Perhaps you can choose to see it as transition time. Turn on happy music to energize you on the way to work and relaxing music to calm you on the way home. You might choose to listen to inspirational programs or nothing at all. Maybe you just want to have some peace and quiet—something you might not get at work or at home.

3. Putting your kids to bed. When you've had a long day and you're ready to rest, putting your children to bed is often the last thing

on your to-do list before you get some time to yourself or time with your spouse. But remember, tucking your little ones in is a ritual that won't be around forever. Savor it. Make it special and sweet. Send your children peacefully into sweet dreams. Make it something you both look forward to.

4. Reading a book or favorite magazine. Words on a page can transport you into another world. Allow yourself to fully experience that world by savoring the moment. Go somewhere comfy. Sit in your favorite chair. Or snuggle up in bed and get lost in the words. Whether reading a novel or something educational, enjoy it.

5. Having a conversation with a friend. How often have you been in a conversation with someone and found that they were doing five other things while in a conversation with you? Whether it is your boss answering calls and checking email while you are trying to get answers you need for a project or your sister not really listening to you because she's distracted watching television, no one likes to feel as though the other person isn't really present. Value conversation. Begin by starting to invite others over or meeting over coffee for nothing more than conversation. Then savor the enjoyment of simply conversing—uninterrupted.

6. Exercising. Even if you don't like to exercise, the truth is it feels good when you finally do! The feeling of satisfaction that comes with knowing you had the discipline to get up and get moving is a confidence booster. In the moment, savor with gratitude the fact that you can exercise. Not everyone is healthy enough to do so.

7. Cooking dinner. I love to cook when I have time. I dislike cooking when I'm rushed. It just becomes another "to-do" to check off the list. Cooking is easier to savor when you don't just think of it as something to check off a list, but instead as an opportunity to be creative, nourish your body, or love your family. It is all in what you tell yourself about what it means to cook.

8. Doing yard work. You can savor time spent planting flowers, mowing grass, and pulling up weeds! Now, I know you may be thinking, "Valorie, you're taking this too far!" But really, I'm not. Being outside is known to boost positive emotion as you interact with nature, and yard work gives you a chance to do that. I'm not saying you have to love it (although I will admit I love pulling up weeds—perhaps there's some sort of emotional symbolism to that), but you can savor it. And it can be even easier to savor when you make it a family activity—an opportunity to work together as a team.

9. Doing nothing. You'd think it would be automatic to savor the times when we have nothing whatsoever to do. Too often, as women, we spend these moments doing everything but savoring! Instead, we spend them thinking about what's next on the to-do list or feeling guilty that we've stopped "doing." If you spend your downtime thinking about everything else you could be doing, it isn't downtime at all. Don't just value "doing." Value "being" too. Value the concept of just being still. It is one of the most productive things you can do to be more effective when it's time to do something again! Savor it.

10. _____

11. _____

12. _____

13. _____

14. _____

15. _____

16. _____

17. _____

18. _____

19. _____

20. _____

Savoring and Self-Esteem

One more interesting fact about savoring: Your ability to savor can be dramatically affected by your self-esteem. Some people actually dampen their own positive emotions when good things happen. Now, some do this because they don't want to appear to gloat or because they are afraid to get their hopes up that more good things might happen. Better to stay cool just in case things go south. Researcher Dr. Brené Brown calls that "foreboding joy," a fear that although things look wonderful right now, they probably won't stay that way. So why get too happy?

However, there is another reason that some women dampen their positive emotions. People who like and value themselves—those who have high self-esteem—view happiness as a state of being that mirrors their own perception of who they are. A woman in this category might say something like, "I am valuable. God loves me and blesses me." To the contrary, a woman who does not like herself or see herself as valuable sees unhappiness as a state of being that she deserves. When positive emotions come, she is more likely to dampen those feelings by downplaying them. She is actually motivated to be unhappy because unhappiness is consistent with who she believes she is.

Now, if the idea of being motivated to be unhappy does not resonate with you, great! But if it does, use this bit of information to recognize that building your sense of worth and value will be an important step in learning to savor the blessings that come to you. Doing so will boost your ability to be happy.

What Are You Telling Yourself?

The key to being able to savor your moments lies in what you tell yourself about the moments you savor, particularly the small experiences. If you tell yourself those moments are unimportant and not worth savoring, that they are simply things you need to get done in order to get through your day, then you will not get through your day with much positive emotion. All of these little moments throughout your day are what create your life, and your approach to them determines the quality of the life you live. Don't buy into the lie that happiness is what finally happens when you meet your goals or hit the jackpot or get married or land the new job. No. A happy life happens in between the big moments. Tell yourself that, and treat your moments accordingly.

In the book of Ecclesiastes, King Solomon warns of this truth again and again. The first time I read Ecclesiastes, I found it a bit sobering—depressing even. But as I have matured in my faith, I see it differently. His warning about "chasing after the wind" is a cautionary word against racing through life trying to accumulate stuff that, in the end, means nothing. Solomon is telling us, "Look, these moments of eating and drinking and working? These moments are your life! Enjoy them. Don't get it mixed up. Family matters. Moments at the dinner table matter. Doing good for others matters!" Take a look at these passages:

> "A person can do nothing better than to eat and drink and find satisfaction in their own toil. This too, I see, is from the hand of God" (Ecclesiastes 2:24).

> "I know that there is nothing better for people than to be happy and do good while they live. That each of them may eat and drink, and find satisfaction in all their toil—this is the gift of God" (Ecclesiastes 3:12-13).

Magnify the Big Moments

We've talked about how important it is to savor the everyday moments, but that doesn't mean the big moments aren't important too. They are. The everyday moments are your journey. The big moments are the destination. They are those moments in which you cross the finish line. And although it is more about the journey than the destination, it would be sad to treat the finish line as though it is no big deal!

Too many women are guilty of this practice, especially those who find themselves on what I call the "achievement treadmill."

If you are constantly moving toward the next big thing, you can dismiss the achievement of the previous big thing. Happy women celebrate milestones and achievement. They acknowledge the strengths of character required to persevere and the relationships that empower them to reach such milestones.

I call it magnifying the big moments. And the first step to magnifying a big moment is acknowledging that it is indeed significant. You landed that new job? Big moment. You just celebrated an anniversary? Big moment. Keep in mind, an anniversary could be a wedding anniversary, friendship anniversary (the anniversary of when you met your BFF, for example!), or a work anniversary (You've persevered and somehow survived three rounds of layoffs? Celebrate!). You finally met a goal that matters to you? Big moment. You're still alive after a bout with breast cancer? Big moment. Finally purchased a home of your own? Big moment. Here's what I suggest you do to magnify your big moments:

1. What moment have you had recently or will you have soon that culminates an important journey in your life? Whether you recently finished a project or met a goal, recognize it as an important milestone.

2. What did it take for you to reach this destination? Write in vivid detail the character traits you had to call on, the friends or even strangers who helped you, the setbacks you bounced back from, and the moments of hope that kept you going. This is a powerful exercise in savoring.

3. What do you feel in this moment? Consciously notice the emotions the moment brings. Do you feel light, like a burden has been lifted? Excited? Grateful? Thrilled? Satisfied? Savor your feelings.

4. How will you celebrate? Choose a meaningful way to celebrate your big moment. Whether it is a party to which you invite friends and family, some time off to bask in the glow of your

accomplishment, or treating yourself or those who helped you to something special, don't forget to celebrate.

Activate This Happiness Trigger!

- Ground yourself in the moment by breathing deeply, feeling your breath enter your nostrils, and filling your lungs and abdomen. Put your feet on the ground. Sense your body and your presence wherever you are.

- Set boundaries around your conversations and activities. This can mean turning off the phone, responding to texts and emails after you've finished the conversation or activity, and resisting the urge to multitask.

- Notice what you feel. Savor moments by consciously raising your awareness of positive emotions.

When You Look Back in Ten Years, What Will You Regret Not Doing?

Points to Ponder

- Making decisions by imagining yourself in the future looking back at the decision can give you a wiser perspective.

- Savoring boosts positive emotion.

- Never make important decisions when you are in a bad mood. Negative emotions narrow your ability to think clearly.

Conversation Starters

- When you look back a decade from now, what will you regret not doing?

- What activities do you rush through that you would like to commit to savoring?

- What holds you back from pursuing the thing you fear you will regret not doing?

I am writing these pages to you from Miami Beach. From where I'm sitting it feels like a tropical oasis. Old Latin jazz plays in the background, and the sounds of birds chirping is so constant I almost don't notice it. Blooming belladonnas are winding around the columns and the signature Florida palm trees that line the patio. It is a blissful setting.

This locale is significant to me for a reason. For years, I've said I love sunny south Florida. I've said I want to spend more time here. I've known the deeply nostalgic and peaceful calm that overtakes me when I am near the ocean. I believe it is rooted in my beginnings. One of my favorite childhood pictures is of me at ten months old, wearing a baby blue bloomer swimsuit and sitting peacefully in the Gulf of Mexico. We were not on vacation. We didn't take vacations back then. We were behind our house—or rather, our trailer—on the beach. And ever since then, the water has always calmed and refreshed my soul. So when it occurred to me that getting away to write could be productive, I thought of the beach. I also thought of the cost. But then my thoughts flowed back to the Mark Twain quote below. It's not the stuff we do that we most regret. It's typically the stuff we didn't do.

> Twenty years from now you will be more disappointed by the things that you didn't do than by the ones you did do. So throw off the bowlines. Sail away from the safe harbor. Catch the trade winds in your sails. Explore. Dream. Discover.

So a few months ago, I made a promise to myself to intentionally *live* more. To do things without overanalyzing. To make more of my dreams realities. That includes the simple dream of spending more time in my favorite place—the beach. Amazingly, during my years in Tallahassee during college, I visited the beach (a mere 45 minutes from campus) just once. While growing up in breathtaking Colorado, I went skiing just a handful of times. While living in Monterey, California, I admired the magnificent coastline from the driver's seat of my car on days I cruised down Highway 101, never stopping to park, get out, and walk the beach.

Why do I bother mentioning these examples? Because if I had it to do over again, I'd spend more time soaking up my environment, creating experiences, and living fully in the richness of the beauty that surrounded me. To be clear, I admired and noticed it, but too often from afar.

What Will You Regret Not Doing?

My love is of environments and being in locations that bring me joy. How about you? What brings you joy? What will you regret *not* doing? Consider the five key areas of your life: relationships, finances, work, health and faith. Fast-forward ten years. Then close your eyes and picture yourself two decades from now. What will you wish you had done? If you are like many women I've coached over the years, your list might look something like this:

- Take a leap of faith
- Live more, worry less
- Eat healthier
- Exercise, even if just 20 minutes a day!
- Stop putting your dream on the back burner
- Travel to an exotic destination
- Work less
- Spend more time with your family

Of course, you may have some other dreams on your list. So make your own. Picturing yourself in the future brings clarity. It helps you weed out what matters from what doesn't. It helps you see what seeds you need to begin planting. I wonder why we too often live as though the life we are living is a trial run—some sort of dress rehearsal. Do we think that somewhere down the road we will get the chance to do it right? *This is it!* Today is it. You will not live this day again. Savor it.

Purpose

Why over-focusing on happiness is a recipe for an unhappy life

---

Decision:

"Happiness is not the sole aim of my existence."

I'd like to tell you that when I first started this book about happiness, the writing was pure joy. It wasn't. In the beginning, I nearly tortured myself. This, unfortunately, is nothing new for me. I have struggled with procrastination since my first term paper was due in seventh grade. But this was different. The subject is happiness, and I should not be unhappy while writing about it!

After a couple of months of frustration, I did some deep soul-searching that led me on a path right back to where I started with my very first book—nine books ago. It was a reminder of something I knew, but had buried beneath striving to write the perfect book on women and happiness: Purpose. At the core, my purpose on this earth is to communicate—to write. And one thing I know for certain: When I write, I am happy. That's because when you find your purpose, you find your joy. Well actually, let me say that a little more clearly: When you find your purpose *and get about the business of living it*, you find your joy.

Your purpose is that thing God created you for. It grounds you. It centers you. It energizes you. It brings you peace to operate in it. You feel like you are doing exactly what you are meant to be doing in the moments when you are engaged fully in it. And most importantly, the world is somehow a bit brighter because of it.

Why Are You Here?

Why are you here? Why are you here on this earth at this time, born into the family you were born into, with your unique gifts and talents, with your experiences? There is indeed a reason you are here. It's your purpose. Some call it your mission. We all have one. Your job is to discover what it is and live it. When you get to the end of your life, don't you want to be able to say, "Mission accomplished"?

It is a sad state of affairs when our mission is fuzzy. We feel a little lost, even if to the rest of the world we look like we know exactly where we are going. I remember winning honors and awards in my previous career field, yet feeling a deep dissatisfaction with my work. Because I was good at my profession, the people around me assumed I was purposeful. But deep down, I knew something was off.

You can have all the external accolades of success, but if there is no purpose to what you are accomplishing, you'll feel a black hole—an empty place in your soul that wants true fulfillment. That true fulfillment comes from knowing you are living on purpose.

One day, while coaching a client who was struggling to articulate her life's mission, a question just rolled off my tongue: *How is someone's life better when they cross your path?* She immediately began describing her mission, "Well, I am a bridge builder who connects people, ideas, and resources. A person's life is better because I help them make the right connection." Just like that. Crystal clear. She articulated her purpose.

Over the years, this powerful question has helped many people understand their purpose. Without a lot of introspection and pondering, answer this question from your gut: How is someone's life better when they cross your path?

We are all here for a reason, leaving the world in some way better than it would otherwise have been without us. The fun part is that we get to accomplish that mission using our own unique gifts, strengths, passions, and experiences. While you are likely not the only person in the world with your particular mission, you are the only one who can accomplish it the way you can. There are people God has uniquely equipped you to impact. They connect with you. They are around you. They are influenced by you. I'm not the only author whose mission is inspiring women to live fulfilling lives, but for some reason right now, something caused you and me to connect. So with you, in this moment, I get to live out my mission.

Who will you connect and live out your purpose with today? My challenge to you is this: Articulate your purpose in one simple sentence.

What Keeps You from Your Purpose?

When I write, I feel joy. The key word there is *when* I write. When I write for joy, just for kicks, the words flow. When I write for an audience, fear kicks in. Judgment. Anxiety. Worry. None of which is the path to happiness. In fact, it is the opposite of what God wants for us. When we live with purpose, we find grace, peace, and joy. So what keeps us from it?

1. Fear you are not enough
2. Fear of rejection
3. Fear of failure
4. Fear of success
5. Making too big a deal of it
6. Perfectionism
7. Believing it is all about us

One of the reasons we hold on to our gifts is because we get caught up in the lie that our gifts are for us—and therefore, they are ours to keep. They are not. Your God-given gifts are for the purpose of blessing others. The more you share your gift, the more valuable it is.

Purpose Includes Unhappy Things

My twenty-ninth birthday had just passed. I barely remember that birthday because my mind was on much more somber and important things—like the fact that my mother had been in the hospital for five weeks. She couldn't walk or eat or use the bathroom without medical assistance. She couldn't see straight or speak without slurring, either. I was the only adult family member who lived in the same city. Relatives came to visit and help, but they would not be there permanently. She would be in the hospital for at least a couple more weeks.

The doctors and rehabilitative staff held a meeting with me. Unbeknownst to me, it was a come-to-Jesus meeting. They had a list of questions. "How are you going to take care of your mother?" the lead doctor asked. "Who will take her to therapy every day? What's your schedule like? Are you planning to move in with her or will she move in with you? We need to teach you how to feed her through the tube in her stomach and how to catheterize her."

You see, happiness cannot be the sole aim of your existense. Happiness is a by-product of a life well lived. That last statement was one I'd been avoiding. And I managed to avoid it until two days before my mother's two-month stay in the hospital ended. Every day, when a nurse came into the room to catheterize my mother, he or she offered to show me how to do it. "Oh, I'm sure her bladder will be back to functioning by the time she is released from the hospital," I insisted. "No need to teach me if it's not necessary." Apparently, the staff was becoming increasingly concerned. So was my mother's sister, Aunt Billie.

Being the God-loving, sweet, but no-nonsense woman she is, Aunt Billie brought the subject up matter-of-factly while we were in the drive-through at KFC one day. "You know you're going to have to learn how to use the catheter," she said gently. I could immediately feel tears well up. It was true. I needed to learn how to do it.

"But I don't want to, Aunt Billie," I said sadly, an aching tightness rising in my throat.

"I know you don't, sweetheart," she said gently. "But you have to."

I sat quietly. I knew she was right. And I knew I didn't want to do it. I was afraid I wouldn't do it right. I was afraid I would forget what to do once I brought Mom home from the hospital. And most of all, I was still struggling to grasp the reality of this new challenge. My 49-year-old mother had been in perfect health at the beginning of the previous month, and now she could not perform the most basic bodily functions most of us take for granted. I was sad. I was scared. I was angry. I was confused. The brain aneurysm and emergency brain surgery had both happened so quickly that I had not yet processed it all or mourned the loss of my mom's health.

Aunt Billie and I sat quietly as I pulled up to the window and handed the friendly cashier some money. "I know," I said. "I'm so sad about all this."

"It's going to be okay," she assured me. "Sometimes in life we have to do stuff we don't want to do."

I believe Aunt Billie's words are a lesson for us all. *Sometimes in life we have to do stuff we don't want to do.* Sometimes we wish our circumstances weren't our circumstances. But they are. And our job in those moments is to step up and live with purpose. In the circumstances of your life that you wish were different, what is your divine assignment? Often, purpose becomes something very specific—an assignment God has given you in this season. Don't miss your assignment. If you do, you miss the point.

That means fulfilling the mission for which you were created. All of us were created for this purpose: to love and serve. Now, loving and serving looks different in each of our lives because the way we love and serve calls on our unique strengths, passions, and experiences. But in the end, fulfilling your purpose means loving and serving others as only you can. That is where your greatest happiness will be found. When you are outside of your purpose, you may find many moments of pleasure or positive emotion, but you will lack the deeper happiness that is joy and satisfaction. That joy and satisfaction is the day-in and day out of a life well-lived—a life purposefully made up of choices that are meaningful to you.

In your life, there will be a few seasons where it seems everything is just right. But in most seasons, there is a trial of some area of your life, whether small or significant. There are tests. There are opportunities to be used by God, to stretch and to grow. If you forego these opportunities and do only what will presumably make you "happy" —in other words, what is easier—you will actually undermine your happiness. A surface life solely composed of pleasure and ease will leave you unfulfilled. True happiness is a deep joy and contentment that comes from knowing that you enjoyed the fun stuff and the good times and you stepped up to your assignment in the difficult ones.

> You see, happiness cannot be the sole aim of your existence. Happiness is a by-product of a life well lived.

I cannot help but think of a scripture from my favorite book in the Bible, James. It is a very short book, but filled with powerful wisdom. James 1:2-3 says, "Consider it pure joy, my brothers and sisters, whenever you face trials of many kinds, because you know that the testing of your faith produces perseverance." It is hard to imagine that trials could bring us joy, but it is true. Have you ever felt the deep satisfaction that comes from persevering through something tough? It is an opportunity to discover who you really are and the strength that God has placed in you. There is no way for you to discover that strength without going through difficulty. In fact, those who have never had to go through much are typically less resilient. And without resilience, it is pretty hard to be happy. Life, after all, is bound to include setbacks and disappointments.

Think back to an instance in which you found yourself in a circumstance you didn't want, yet you rose to the occasion and found satisfaction in your ability to do so. You completed your "divine assignment." Got a specific instance in mind? Now, imagine for a moment that instead of stepping up to the plate, you missed your assignment. You did what was easier in the moment rather than what was purposeful long-term. How would you feel about your decision now? What regrets might you have? How would it have impacted a relationship? Would you be happier with yourself or disappointed in yourself?

Happiness Requires Resilience, Resilience Requires Adversity

Your overall well-being is increased when you know that you can handle whatever comes your way. With God, all things are indeed possible. In fact, one of my favorite scriptures is this: "My grace is sufficient for you, for my power is made perfect in weakness" (2 Corinthians

12:9). You don't have to have the answers or the strength, but if you can surrender the situation to God and allow him to give you the grace to persevere, you will survive and even thrive through adversity.

> True happiness is a deep joy and contentment
> that comes from knowing that you enjoyed the
> fun stuff and the good times and you stepped
> up to your assignment in the difficult ones.

I was sad that day in the car with Aunt Billie. I was scared. But once I surrendered to reality, I stepped into that season of my life with clarity of purpose. My mission during that season was not so much about inspiring women to live fulfilling lives. It was about inspiring and caring for one woman in particular: my mother. I cannot imagine doing anything other than what I chose to do. If for some crazy reason I had, I am not sure how I could have lived with myself. Was I happy about doing it? No. Did I think it was fair? No. Did I wish she had not become disabled? Of course! But I learned to deal with our new normal. And in doing so, we had many joyful moments in the midst of a trial. We enjoyed moments of humor, like when my mother would bump into shelves in the grocery store trying to use the scooter-like shopping cart. We enjoyed moments of hope, like when she managed one day to walk slowly down the driveway to the mailbox by herself, a first that took several months to achieve. And we enjoyed moments of achievement, like when the doctor finally agreed that her swallowing was good enough to remove the feeding tube, a miracle in light of the fact that we'd been told there was a 90 percent chance she'd never swallow again. Going through these things together brought us closer and closeness brings joy.

As for my mother, her journey remains one of perseverance. But she says she is happier now than she was before the aneurysm. She now lives in the town where she grew up, near her siblings, nieces and nephews, and even great-great nieces and nephews—something that makes her quite happy. Interestingly, research tells us that it is not circumstances that make us happy anyway. Studies show that those who suffer setbacks, such as a health challenge or accident that leads to a disability, typically bounce back within two years to a level of happiness very near to the happiness level they experienced prior to the setback. That's resilience. You can't be happy without it.

Caution: Every Decision Cannot Be About What Makes You "Happy" Right Now

Our culture today seems to be filled with examples of people making decisions purely based on "right now" happiness. And those decisions often lead to long-term unhappiness. I want to challenge you as you are faced with constant decisions in your life—relationship decisions, health choices, money matters, and career choices. **Ask yourself this: A year from now, or even ten years from now, what choice will I wish I had made?** *Make that choice.* Whether you are tempted to rack up credit card debt for something you can't afford or contemplating divorce for "irreconcilable differences," remember that long-term happiness sometimes requires delayed gratification. That means you may have to endure the discipline of short-term frustration for the reward of long-term well-being. If happiness becomes the sole aim of your existence, your life will be dominated by pleasure rather than purpose. And that is a recipe for an unhappy life. But if divine purpose leads your decision, true happiness is sure to be yours!

Activate This Happiness Trigger!

- Articulate your purpose in a simple sentence. It should answer the question, "How is someone's life better when they cross your path?"

- When faced with unwanted circumstances, ask, "What's my divine assignment here?"

- When making a difficult decision, avoid making decisions based purely on what makes you happy now. Instead ask, "Ten years from now, what will I wish I had done?"

Conclusion
Be Happy *While*, Not Just Happy *When*

Although I didn't know what to call it at the time, my first bout with the depression came when I was about 15 years old. My parents had separated. We lost our home. We lived 1,500 miles from our family. I was deeply sad. I was also embarrassed. So I didn't tell my friends we'd lost our home and I didn't talk much about my parents' pending divorce. I knew people who didn't let their kids hang around kids from broken homes and I feared the sting of rejection. When my head hit the pillow at night and there was nothing to distract me, my grief was overwhelming. I tried to go to sleep, but flashbacks of happier times with my parents kept me awake. We used to have dinner together every night and now when I closed my eyes at night, I would always see us there at the dinner table together. Lying in bed, the emotion burned my neck and throat as I tried to hold in my tears. But I couldn't. The tears streamed onto my pillow until finally they lulled me to sleep. Every night, I kept my sobs quiet. I didn't want my mother to know just how sad I was. I wanted my family back together. I wanted my home and my neighborhood back. But that wish was beyond my control, so I focused on what I could control—school and my social life. I believe it was my close friendships, church, extracurricular activities, and sports that saved me. I felt a part of something bigger than me, and while that didn't entirely keep me from being angry and disappointed, it gave me enough light to keep me from sinking into a deep, dark hole.

If you've ever struggled with depression, you know that once it comes, it likes to revisit. My experience was not the exception. In my

mid-twenties, depression hit me again. On the outside I looked successful and even happy. I ran a successful business, owned my own home,
and had family who loved me. I was healthy, fun to be around…and
sad. This time when depression hit, I recognized it. I found a thera-
pist. I did some deep soul-searching. I had questions. *Who am I? Why
am I here? What difference do I want to make in the world?* I prayed for
answers. In time, they came. And without knowing what to call them,
I began activating my happiness triggers. I discovered my purpose and
passion and have pursued it ever since. I found ways to serve my community. I sought out like-minded friendships and nurtured them. I
began to travel and take vacations. With each step, I felt empowered
and my spirits lifted.

In my mid-thirties, I faced the most painful season of my life and
my biggest fear—a divorce of my own. I had to start my life over. When
depression attempted to attack again, I was equipped for the fight! This
time my faith was stronger than ever and I had just finished graduate
school in applied positive psychology at the University of Pennsylvania.
I'd spent hundreds of hours studying well-being and resilience from the
foremost researchers in the field. Now, I needed to put my knowledge
to work in my own life. Would it work? There was only one way to
find out. I used every single happiness trigger in this book, and I didn't
just survive the attack in my life, *I thrived through it*. When fear whispered, "You failed. You have no right to write books or speak or coach
anybody anymore!" I talked back to my fears: "My purpose didn't end
because my life isn't perfect. I will glean purpose from my pain and it'll
make me a more compassionate woman and a stronger writer." When
uncertainty shouted, "Your best years are behind you," my faith assured
me, "Your life has just begun! This turning point will usher you into a
new and happier season."

I chose resilience. You can too. Abraham Lincoln famously said,
"Most people are about as happy as they make up their minds to be."
Have the faith to believe happiness is possible no matter what. Know
this: Challenges *will* come. You may not be happy *about* what happens,
but you can find happiness *in spite* of what happens. I learned that from
the apostle Paul who said, "I have learned the secret of being content in

any and every situation, whether well fed or hungry, whether living in plenty or in want. I can do all this through him who gives me strength." I believe it was God's grace that empowered me to take charge of my happiness in the face of trying times. I know firsthand that happiness triggers work—not simply because research says so, but because I have seen them work in my own life. And I trust that as you move forward, they will work in yours.

My life is happier than it has ever been—not because I have everything I want, but because **I've learned that I won't be happy when I get what I want if I don't learn to be happy while waiting for what I want.** The destinations we desire arrive in brief moments. Most of life is spent getting to the destination. Learn to be happy as you journey through both challenges and triumphs, and you'll discover the secret to a happy life.

Love,

Valorie

Pay It Forward

Top 10 Happiness Lessons to Teach Your Girls and Young Women

Now that you are equipped with the tools of happiness, pay it forward! I've created a Top 10 list to make it easy for you to talk to the young women in your life about what it really takes to be happy in today's world. You can use this list to strike up conversation with them and start to influence how they think about their own happiness. Each lesson includes a question and some thoughts you can use as a conversation starter. Who are the young women you want to influence?

1. **Don't just plan your career; plan your personal life.**
   What do you want your personal life to look like ten years from now? Set goals for your career, but also set goals for what you want personally. If marriage is the goal, when you are of age, date only those whom you would actually consider marrying—those who share your goals for family and spiritual life and have a shared vision you want to live out. And choose friends who share your values. Be there for them, but be sure you choose friends who will also be there for you.

2. **Nobody on a magazine cover really looks like that!**
   Who do you tend to compare yourself to? Stop making upward comparisons to women who don't actually exist. *Every* magazine photo is airbrushed to make the model look flawless. In real life, she has blemishes too! Embrace your unique beauty.

3. **You have a purpose. Your job in life is to find it and live it.**
   How is someone's life better because they cross your path? Every day, do something to brighten someone else's day. There is a reason you were created. You have gifts, talents, passion, and

experiences that can make this world a better place. You are not meant to hold on to them, but to use them for good.

4. **It's okay to fail. It's not trying that you'll regret.**

   What are you afraid to try for fear you might fail? It's not okay to let fear keep you from trying. When you fail, learn the lesson. Use it next time. The happiest women live without regrets. They are bold enough to go for what they want. They know the secret to success is to keep trying until they succeed.

5. **"No man is a good catch who is not madly in love with you." – Pearl Cleage**

   Does he treat you as the valuable woman you are? A man's success and good looks are not what make him a good catch! How he treats you, his character, emotional stability, and faith do. Don't settle. Don't chase a guy. The one you are meant to be with will find you and he will know he's found a good thing. You'll know by how he treats you. He won't risk letting you slip away.

6. **Don't say anything about yourself that you don't want to be true.**

   Your words matter. Never speak words that you don't want to come true: "I can't." "I'm stupid." "Nobody loves me." Speak only words that give life to your dreams: "I have what it takes." "I can." "I'm good enough." Optimism breeds happiness!

7. **Buy experiences, not "stuff."**

   What's one thing you would like to have the money to do? Happy women live below their means and aim to be debt-free. While your friends are penching pennies to pay off credit cards and loans, you'll have the freedom to save money, give some away, and spend some on experiences that bring real happiness—a night out with friends, a fun trip, or dance or photography lessons to teach you something new.

8. **Talk to your family more than you email and text them.**

   Texting and emailing is great for touching bases and sharing information. But make it a habit to actually talk to the people who matter. Happy women connect face-to-face, where they can touch, see, and truly be with a person. You can't build a strong relationship in 140 characters or less.

9. **Listen to that still, small voice.**

   Have you ever felt your inner voice telling you something, but just ignored it? When? God speaks in a whisper, a nudge in your spirit that guides you in the right direction. Don't ignore that still, small voice. Trust your ability to hear from God. He gives you that "gut instinct," that "intuition." It is divine intelligence. Don't discount it or ignore it. It is your secret weapon! And if you are ever afraid you are wrong about it, trust that God will let you know and redirect your steps.

10. **Play!**

    What do you like to do purely for the joy of it? Your life is a gift. Enjoy it! Everything doesn't have to be about reaching goals and getting results. Sometimes, you just need to stop and play! Always keep your "inner kid" alive.

Personalized Action Plans

Single Without Children

- Don't idealize marriage.
- Make a list of ten good things about being single. It's your single girl gratitude list!
- Host a get-together. Invite friends you haven't seen in a while and people you'd like to get to know better.
- Take a trip. Where have you been thinking of going?
- Be intentional about being around people. Get a roommate if you don't like living alone. If you work alone from home, get out and have lunch, go to professional association events, and find a way to serve.
- Don't wait for a knight in shining armor to save you financially.
- Buy your own home. It can be a great pre-marriage investment. Keep it after you get married—rent it out and pay it off.

Single Moms

- Live near family or close friends. Place a high value on your support system. This means think twice before moving somewhere you don't have a network
- Accept and tell the truth to your children. Don't belittle your ex, but also don't make excuses for him if he is not involved. Speak the truth in love and support your children as they learn to handle the truth.
- Do your best and accept that you can only be a mom, not mom and dad. Seek trusted male role models to provide a fatherly influence if the father is not involved.
- Take regular breaks. If you can afford a sitter, get one and

give yourself a weekly rest. Or trade with another mom or family member.

- When others offer to help, accept their offer! And if they don't ask and you need help, *ask*.

- Have a "play date" with your kids once a week. Let them pick the activity. Lighten up, laugh, and have a ball!

- When you tuck your children in to bed, start a gratitude conversation with them: What were the three best things about today?

Empty Nesters

- What have you been putting off? Do it! Make a plan. Set a timeline. Enjoy!

- Take up a new hobby.

- Engage your senses by learning something new. Take a class in Italian, learn to play the piano, or start painting and writing for the first time in your life.

- Take a family trip with your adult children.

- Take a girlfriends' trip to a fun destination. Make it an annual adventure if you want, or join a travel club.

- If you are married, rekindle the romance with your spouse. Take a second honeymoon to celebrate this new phase of life together.

- Ask yourself, "What am I looking forward to in the next three, five, and ten years?"

Married Working Moms

- Make your marriage a priority. Sit down with your spouse to schedule time together daily (even if just 30 minutes) and weekly.

- Agree that if one of you is swamped at work, the other will pick up the slack at home. Discuss this now rather than in the midst of a hectic week.

- Let the kids plan "play dates" for the whole family. Whether it's a night in with pizza and board games, flag football, or a trip to the amusement park, make "play" a tradition in your entire family (mom and dad included!).

- Make love to your husband today—and forget about the dishes when you're at it! It's good for you and your marriage and keeps you connected. I know you're busy, but when the sex goes, the marriage follows.

- Take a break. Talk to your spouse about a break once a week to let you relax and breathe—even if just for a couple of hours. When would be the best day of the week and time?

- When you tuck your children into bed, start a gratitude conversation with them: What were the three best things about today?

Stay-at-Home Moms

- Write down your own personal definition of happiness. How do you define "having it all"?

- Connect with other women. Have other moms over while your kids play, plan a girls' night out once a month, and call to check in with friends and old colleagues. Don't lose touch with the outside world!

- Savor your season with your children. Take pictures. Make scrapbooks together. Ten years from now, what do you most want to remember doing with your kids?

- Let go of perfection in pursuit of connection. The house doesn't have to be perfect before you play with your kids. *Enjoy them.* This time is precious.

- When the kids are big enough, find a volunteer or service project to do together. Even let the kids choose a cause that is meaningful to them.

- When your kids come home from school, ask them, "What's the best thing that happened at school today?"

DINKs (Double Income No Kids)

- Focus on building a strong relationship with your spouse. Don't let work overwhelm your evenings and weekends. Make each other the priority when you're at home.

- Work out together. What do you both like to do? It's a great way to stay connected, release some endorphins, and stay healthy.

- Pray together. Connecting spiritually leads to a deeper, more fulfilling marriage.

- Have a no-tech period in the evenings, even if just for a half hour. Put the phone away. The texts can wait. Catch up with each other. Look each other in the eye. Connect.

- Aim to live on just one income. Double income has become a necessity in too many households, often because couples pursue a lifestyle that *requires* two incomes. But if you want a fast-track to building a nest egg, living below your means, and being able to bless others, aim to live on one of your incomes and use the second income for savings and special treats such as vacations.

- Make a list of things you want to experience before you have kids (if you are planning to have them). Savor this season of your marriage. Do the things you won't be able to do during your children's early years. Enjoy!

Notes

HAPPY WOMEN READ INTRODUCTIONS!

1. Betsey Stevenson and Justin Wolfers, "The Paradox of Declining Female Happiness." *American Economic Journal* 1, no. 2 (August 1, 2009):190-225.

2. Meghan Casserly, "Is 'Opting Out' the New American Dream for Working Women?" *Forbes*, September 12, 2012, http://www.forbes.com/sites/meghancasserly/2012/09/12/is-opting-out-the-new-american-dream-for-working-women/.

3. "Depression in Women: Understanding the Gender Gap," Mayo Clinic, last modified January 19, 2013, http://www.mayoclinic.com/health/depression/MH00035.

4. Martin E.P. Seligman, *Learned Optimism* (New York: Vintage Books, 1990).

5. Selena Rezvani, "For Women, It's *Really* Lonely at the Top," *Washington Post*, May 28, 2010, http://views.washingtonpost.com/leadership/panelists/2010/05/for-women-its-really-lonely-at-the-top.html.

6. Sonja Lyubomirsky, *The How of Happiness* (New York: Penguin Press, 2008).

7. Ibid.

8. Daniel Kahneman and Angus Deaton, "High Income Improves Evaluation of Life but Not Emotional Well-Being," *Proceedings of the National Academy of Science of the United States of America* 107, no. 38 (August 4, 2010): 16489–93, http://www.pnas.org/content/107/38/16489.

HAPPINESS TRIGGER #2: SMILE!

1. L.A. Harker and D. Keltner, "Expressions of Positive Emotion in Women's College Yearbook Pictures and Their Relationship to Personality and Life Outcomes Across Adulthood," *Journal of Personality and Social Psychology*, 2001.

2. E.L. Abel and M.L. Kruger, "Smile Intensity in Photographs Predicts Longevity," *Psychological Science*, 2010.

3. Melinda Werner, "Smile! It Could Make You Happier," *Scientific American*, October 2009.

HAPPINESS TRIGGER #3: SERVICE

1. Seligman, *Learned Optimism.*

HAPPINESS TRIGGER #4: FINANCIAL SAVVY

1. Shaunti Feldhahn, *For Women Only* (Colorado Springs, Multnomah Books, 2004).

2. Sandra Tsing Loh, "Rich Wives, Poor Husbands," *The Atlantic Monthly*, October 2012.

HAPPINESS TRIGGER #5: GRATITUDE

1. Robert A. Emmons, *Thanks! How the New Science of Gratitude Can Make You Happier* (New York: Houghton Mifflin, 2007).

HAPPINESS TRIGGER #6: CONNECTION

1. "Living Alone? You're Not Alone," CBSNews, May 20, 2012, http://www.cbsnews.com/8301-3445_162-57437837/live-alone-youre-not-alone/.

2. Miller McPherson, Lynn Smith-Lovin, and Matthew E. Brashears, "Social Isolation in America: Changes in Core Discussion Networks over Two Decades," *American Sociological Review* 71, no. 353 (2006).

3. James H. Fowler and Nicholas A. Christakis, "Dynamic Spread of Happiness in a Large Social Network: Longitudinal Analysis over 20 Years in the Framingham Heart Study," *British Medical Journal*, (December 5, 2008), doi: 10.1136/bmj.a2338.

HAPPINESS TRIGGER #7: FLOW

1. Mihaly, Csikszentmihalyi, *Flow: The Psychology of the Optimal Experience* (New York: Harper, 1990).

HAPPINESS TRIGGER #8: PLAY

1. Alan Krueger, "Are We Having More Fun Yet? Categorizing and Evaluating Changes in Time Allocation," *Brookings Papers on Economic Activity* 2, (2007), http://www.brookings.edu/~/media/projects/bpea/fall%202007/2007b_bpea_krueger.pdf .

2. Stuart Brown, "Play Science—The Patterns of Play," National Institute for Play website, www.nifplay.org.

3. George MacKerron and Susana Mourato, "Happiness Is Greater in Natural Environments," *Global Environmental Change* (May 20, 2013), doi: 10.1016/j.gloenvcha.2013.03.010.

4. Tom Rath, *Well Being: The Five Essential Elements* (New York: Gallup Press, 2010).

HAPPINESS TRIGGER #9: RELAXATION

1. Andrea Thompson, "Why Women Worry So Much," *Live Science*, September 28, 2007, http://www.livescience.com/9535-women-worry.html.

HAPPINESS TRIGGER #11: MOVEMENT

1. N. Hellmich, N. "Good Mood Can Run a Long Time After Workout," *USA Today*, June 2, 2009, http://usatoday30.usatoday.com/news/health/weightloss/2009-06-02-exercise-mood_N.htm?csp=34.

2. "Exercise and Depression," Harvard Medical School, retrieved July 7, 2013, http://www.health.harvard.edu/newsweek/Exercise-and-Depression-report-excerpt.htm.

HAPPINESS TRIGGER #12: SAVORING

1. Brene Brown, *Daring Greatly: How the Courage to Be Vulnerable Transforms the Way We Live, Love, Parent, and Lead* (New York, Gotham: 2012).

Discover Your Happiness
Triggers for FREE at

www.valorieburton.com.

...and here are five more smart things you can do at valorieburton.com:

- Join thousands of subscribers to Valorie's free weekly e-newsletter.

- Take free assessments and read tons of free articles to help you get unstuck and be unstoppable!

- Check out Valorie's speaking schedule.

- Find upcoming dates for The CaPP Institute's Coach Training Intensives and coach certification programs.

- Connect with Valorie on her blog, leave her comments, and interact with other readers.

To learn more about Harvest House books and
to read sample chapters, log on to our website:

www.harvesthousepublishers.com

HARVEST HOUSE PUBLISHERS
EUGENE, OREGON